Selling Strategically

Best wishes

Selling Strategically

A 21st-Century Playbook

Terry Barge

Sales Strategist for
High-Performing Sales Teams

DAGMAR
MIURA
LOS ANGELES

Dagmar Miura
Los Angeles
www.dagmarmiura.com

First published 2016

ISBN: 978-1-942267-13-3

This book is dedicated to my lovely wife, Ellie, who has been my constant encourager, supporter, and advisor throughout the complete process of producing this book

Contents

CHAPTER ONE

Introduction

"Change is the only constant in life".
—Heraclitus, Greek philosopher

For the past twenty years I have been fortunate to have worked with thousands of salespeople and many world-class organisations in more than fifty countries across five continents.

This extraordinary experience has provided me with unique insight into what it takes to be effective as a strategic salesperson operating in the post-recession business-to-business sales environment.

A Rude Awakening

At an advanced sales training workshop a few years ago, my fellow participants and I were asked by the workshop leader to introduce ourselves and say how many years we had been working in sales. He wrote each of our responses on the flip chart, then flipped over the page and moved on.

The focus of the next module was a group review of the important changes that we were experiencing in our individual sales situations. The workshop leader asked us about the changes in our marketplace – our customers, our competitors and our own organisation as well.

We fell over one another, filling the flip chart with our responses.

We told him that customers had become more demanding and competitors more aggressive. Our own organisations had set even tougher sales targets. We all looked around the room and nodded affably to one another, well satisfied with our communal feedback. It was tough out there!

It became very clear, very quickly that everything seemed to be changing at an all-new pace, and that all of us were confronting significantly more sales challenges than ever before.

The workshop leader then summarised our responses in a very searching way: "So, if, as you say, your customers are changing, your competitors are changing and your own organisations are changing, just **how much are *you* changing** to meet what appear to be some very formidable demands being made on you by your marketplace?"

We looked at one another once again, slightly baffled by his question. Our brows furrowed and the silence seemed deafening as we all searched for some kind of intelligent response. None came.

Turning back the flip chart to the page that contained our introductions, he then added to our professional embarrassment.

He turned to me and said, "Terry, you've been selling for almost 10 years, right?" I nodded in agreement. He then delivered his coupe de grace: "Is that 10 years of continuously developing and honing your sales skills to match the daunting changes in your marketplace, or is it just the same old one year, ten times over?"

For some reason, I felt both awkward and annoyed. I searched for an answer but came up with nothing of any real substance.

His point was impactful and the message he conveyed so simply yet so powerfully still resonates with me today. The bottom line of his message was incisive: "You are already losing if you allow yourself and your skills to be left behind as your marketplace changes and moves on".

Upon reflection, it seems my mind-set at that point in time mirrored Einstein's now legendary definition of insanity: "doing the same thing over and over again and expecting different results".

In this book we will be focusing almost exclusively on a significant change in sales perspective – **from transactional selling to strategic selling.** This "change" is not so much about core consulting skills (which, while important, are not the point of this book) as it is about using these skills in a more appropriate and effective way.

We will always need to use our full range of consulting skills in our everyday interactions with customers. If these pivotal communication skills are not in place, it becomes virtually impossible to enjoy a rapport with anybody, whether in a business or a personal setting.

Rapport is the foundation of effective personal relationships – however, it is certainly not sufficient on its own, to build the levels of credibility and trust that drive that all-important competitive advantage.

I am convinced that even if you are the world's greatest practitioner of consulting skills but are consulting with the wrong customers, talking to the wrong people, asking the wrong questions about the wrong issues, you are going to lose far more business than you will ever win.

A Note for the Reader

At various points in the book, you will be offered Playbook activities designed to help you to translate the different categories of knowledge into "live" sales action. To make these Playbook activities easier to reference, I have also placed them, in sequence, at the end of the book.

CHAPTER TWO

The Times They Are A-Changing

> "Business life is no longer as predictable as it was a generation ago.... Changes have all combined to create the sensation of careening at a furious pace through the twists and turns of the economy without roadmaps, steering wheels or brakes".
> —Cohen and Bradford, *Influence Without Authority*

The financial crisis of 2007–2008 is viewed by many financial experts as the worst financial crisis since the Great Depression of the 1930s. It continues to have a severe impact on all marketplaces.

The crisis began within the banking sector and resulted in a deep and intense recession – which in turn resulted in a serious decrease in access to credit and financing for both businesses and individuals.

Businesses especially need access to credit – to finance today's business operations and to invest in tomorrow's business plans and projects. Another important feature of this recession that we should note is that it has been experienced by nearly all businesses across all sectors.

So how do this recession and its aftershock impact the way we need to sell? Here's how one commentator describes the current marketplace and some of the recessionary fallout.

> "In virtually all markets, demand has shrunk, there is immense pressure on suppliers to reduce prices, markets are more focused on buying on price, and profit margins are squeezed. The fear of downfall as a result of recessionary pressures has led, and continues to lead, to a fierce slashing of budgets."
> —Julia Cupman of B2B International, *Effective Marketing Strategies for a Recession*

These factors have conspired to turn our traditional selling marketplace virtually upside down. As a result, every person involved in sales at any level has had to grapple with new challenges. How do we sell effectively in this new climate, where sales opportunities are less plentiful because shrunken budgets and cautious attitudes continue to have a significant effect on investment decisions?

Buyers Have Changed

The attitude and motivation of many customers have developed significantly during the recent recession. Their buying mindset has changed and their procurement processes reflect a new way of buying – with which salespeople have to come to terms if they want to remain effective and successful.

> "Buyers have evolved. Overwhelmed with an increasing number of choices, buyers are no longer willing to wait patiently for sales reps to make that perfect pitch".
> —Qvidian's *"2015 State of Sales Execution Report"*

In a recent *Harvard Business Review* article, we can see even more evidence of this trend in how customers and their buying approach have evolved:

"A recent Corporate Executive Board study of more than 1,400 B2B customers found that those customers completed, on average, nearly 60 percent of a typical purchasing decision – researching solutions, ranking options, setting requirements, benchmarking pricing, and so on – before even having a conversation with a supplier".
—Brent Adamson, Matthew Dixon and Nicholas Toman

These unprecedented changes are transforming the traditional sales environment and challenging sales professionals throughout the world.

The Selling Challenge

Pursuing and winning sales opportunities is and will always be the top priority for all salespeople. However, the continuing effects of the lingering recession mean that the kind of sales opportunities we describe as "low-hanging fruit" no longer remain in anything like the quantity needed for survival – and certainly not if revenue growth and profitability are to remain realistic objectives.

This new scenario has created a new powerful and compelling situation. If there are not enough sales opportunities coming from traditional sources to fill our pipeline, how do we intend to hit our sales targets which are still set for revenue and profit growth?

Here's how McDonald, Rogers and Woodburn describe some of the early customer and supplier actions being taken to address this particular issue.

> "We see companies starting to build models of account attractiveness, matching their resources to the profit and status potential of any given customer or prospect. We also witness increasing professionalism among purchasers and decision making units in buying companies as they evaluate the longer-term value offered by suppliers (the quality of products, processes and people) rather than solely the price deal".
> McDonald, Rogers and Woodburn, *Key Customers – How to Manage Them Profitably*

What Needs to Happen?

What will an effective salesperson need to focus on in the post-recession marketplace?

First, we have to accept and embrace this new sales paradigm, and seriously reflect on how we can be more sales-effective going forward.

What we are really seeing is a clear movement away from the traditional deal-by-deal, transactional relationship with customers. Transactional selling has as its primary focus selling products as commodities, with discounting as the primary source of perceived customer value. This kind of relationship is often described as a "vendor" or even an "order taker".

This evolution in sales approach points clearly away from the transactional approach, towards one which is far more strategic and based on longer-term, sustainable value. This kind of relationship is unmistakably headed in the direction of the classic "trusted adviser".

> "The business revolution is sweeping away many of the traditional ways of working, of interacting with customers. If we don't change, if we don't embrace the future, we will be left behind".
> —Larry Wilson, *Stop Selling, Start Partnering*

CHAPTER THREE

Being Strategic

"Selling today in the corporate sector takes place in
an environment that is volatile, uncertain, complex and
ambiguous. As never before, the sales professional must
react and adapt to the nature and change in business".
— "Buyers' View of Salespeople" 2012, TACK International

Oxford Dictionary defines *strategic* as "relating to the identification of long term aims and interests and the means of
achieving them".

When I ask salespeople what comes to mind when they
consider the word "strategic", they usually come up with
phrases such as:

- "Having a longer-term view"
- "Seeing the bigger picture"
- "Having a plan of action"
- "Having a focus on the future"
- "Linking the present with the future"
- "Understanding a customer's future plans"
- "Possessing competitive insight"

These kinds of definitions may sound familiar, and

experienced salespeople may already sense some similarities between selling strategically and the more established sales practice of Key Account management. However, there are some key differences between the newer paradigm of selling strategically and the more traditional Key Account management approach.

Key Account Management tends to be a sales process supported by Key Account Plans where the *sellers'* perspective of the customer environment is the primary focus.

In Key Account Management, the customer's business situation will play a pivotal role; however, it does so with the principle objective of enabling the salesperson to locate and then pursue sales opportunities. In contrast, selling strategically views the customer as **an equal partner** in the sales process – mutual value and collaborative partnerships are at the heart of the strategic salesperson's approach.

In research carried out by TACK International, buyers were asked what attributes they most valued in suppliers' salespeople.

"In order of importance, respondents rated the relationship-based approach, value delivered and product and service performance as the elements they most value in sales people/supplier relationships. Interestingly...price and cost savings were lower down the list".
—Buyers' View of Salespeople, 2012

Reassuringly, the evolution from a transactional sales approach to one which is more strategic and value-based is not so much about a completely new suite of skills but much more about a change of perspective and attitude on the part of the salesperson.

"Strategic thinking starts with your basic skills and considers how best to use them".
—Dixit and Nalebuff, *Thinking Strategically*

Changing Gear

So, as we covered in the Introduction, today's salesperson will still need to be an effective practitioner of rapport-building skills, such as open and closed questioning, positive body language and active listening.

The change of gear will be a different mindset and transformed perspective that steers how these core skills are applied in the post-recessionary selling environment. Let's call this new salesperson the Sales Strategist.

The Sales Strategist's perspective is based around a much higher level of commercial acumen, political understanding and competitive insight. Without a strategic perspective we will not be able to deliver the sustainable, longer-term value expected by key customers.

If transactional salespeople live in "the foothills" of the customer's organisation, with a limited vision of its business situation, Sales Strategists live much higher up "the mountain" – **they see more, they understand more and most important, they win more.**

Let me give you an example of how one account manager realised how important it was to seek out this "higher level" of insight.

I was working with a group of account managers from a major telecoms company. We were creating sales value propositions. The power of SVPs is almost totally based around the quality of information the salesperson possesses about the customer's business situation, and the confidence that the information is coming from the most informed people. As usual, I was enacting "live" sales situations to test the effectiveness of the SVPs being produced by the group.

At the conclusion of the one-day workshop, I asked each member of the group to tell me what they had learnt from the day. The feedback was pretty positive overall, but one response in particular comes to mind.

We had used one of this participant's "live" customer situations, and the SVP his group had produced was above average. However, it still lacked a certain persuasive quality, due to a lack of some key customer information.

His feedback was different than the rest of the group's: "I have to go back to my customer and find different people to talk to and ask them different questions".

There was nothing wrong with his interpersonal skills. His lack of effectiveness was all about his peripheral vision. He was in the foothills, and he realised that he needed to climb higher and apply those skills more strategically.

For him, the Sales Strategist's mindset was just beginning to kick in.

So what were some of the things he needed to find out?

- How does my customer define and measure success?
- What are the external marketplace factors which are impeding the achievement of success?
- What internal initiatives are being implemented to improve its performance?

Interestingly, our account manager had also said he needed to talk to different people. Who were they?

They were the individuals who controlled or who had some influence over the customer's strategic decision making process.

Our account manager had also realised that a key to his success was the identification of those individuals who had organisational power – both formal and informal.

- Who are the people who are authorized to make strategic decisions?
- Who are the "trusted lieutenants" whose advice and opinions they value?
- What level of rapport and credibility had been developed with each of them?
- What level of rapport and credibility had competitors developed with each of them?

That last point seems to indicate that the Sales Strategist

also needs to have a clear appreciation of the competitive landscape as well.

Absolutely! How can competitive advantage and solution differentiation be created if there is little insight about the competitive landscape?

A key building block in the creation of an effective sales strategy is the depth of insight we have of the competitive environment.

- With whom are we competing?
- What is the customer's level of satisfaction with our competitors?
- What are their strengths and weaknesses?
- At what level of the organisation are they focusing – operational, management or executive?
- What is our level of competitive advantage?

Without these answers about our strategic sales environment, we will lack the insight and versatility necessary to produce sustainable and longer-term strategic value for the customer and for our own organisations.

Intelligence Is All

TACK International's research indicates the absolute need for increased levels of commercial acumen, political understanding and competitive insight.

> "The lack of market predictability constantly tests the business acuity and understanding of sales professionals of the markets in which they operate".
> —Buyers' View of Salespeople, 2012

Here is one of the most outstanding examples I have ever seen of the lengths to which an account manager went in order to understand the strategic goal and objectives of his customer.

I was working with a UK client in the beverage market. They sell their niche product to restaurants, bars, nightclubs and hotels, and also into the higher-value market, like supermarkets, national pub chains and large food wholesalers.

During a strategic planning workshop, the various teams were working with a selection of "live" customers and sales opportunities. One of the key account executives asked if we could work on one of his prospects, a national chain of around 600 pubs. He had an opportunity to pitch for shelf space for his product across the whole chain. The revenue value ran into the millions.

During the workshop, the group had discussed the issue of being strategic in their approach, and the need to move from a commoditised product approach to a longer-term, value-based partnership. As part of the workshop process, he used these principles to prepare his initial sales plan and his draft "pitch".

Six weeks later, I met the group again to review their progress, listen to their successes and provide assistance if and where they needed more help. When the young account executive's turn came, he told a quite remarkable story. He filled us in about his sales opportunity and went on to say that he was competing for the pub chain's business with three other internationally recognised brands.

Each company had been given 30 minutes to make their pitch to a panel of five senior executives from the pub chain. Following the 30-minute presentation, there would be a question and answer session, and then within five days the final decision would be made.

In advance of his presentation, he had decided to polish his pitch. To make sure it was as strategic as possible, he spent a whole weekend watching and rewatching the pub chain's last shareholder's meeting on YouTube. He told us that he wanted to get as clear an understanding as possible of his prospect's longer-term goals and objectives, and also its corporate values.

He then proceeded to connect his own company's goals, objectives and values to those of his customer. He told us that he wanted to create a very strong message that emphasised the strategic value of a long-term partnership between the two companies. With this approach in mind, he consciously decided that his actual product was going to play a supporting role in his pitch.

At the conclusion of the 30 minutes, the executives told him that he had answered all their questions – and they asked for extra time to start discussing his ideas for implementing his proposal!

He was successful, mainly because he "got the message" and moved away from the product-based approach that his competitors took. He changed his mind-set and moved to a much more strategic approach.

He demonstrated genuine, longer-term value based around shared goals, shared values and a clear understanding of what success meant to the customer – the foundations of a true value-based partnership.

The Key Roles of the Sales Strategist

So what are the key attributes and skills that will enable sales professionals to evolve from the redundant transactional sales approach to that of the Sales Strategist?

Let's start with the four distinct roles that define the profile of a successful Sales Strategist. Sales professionals will need to operate consistently and effectively in each of these roles if sustained levels of sales performance are going to be achieved in the post-recessionary era.

The four roles are:

1. Business Consultant
2. Relationship Manager
3. Competitor Analyst
4. Solutions Provider

Together, these four roles make up the core capabilities that enable Sales Strategists to operate far more effectively and successively than their transactional counterparts – because they focus on the business, political and competitive insight that is essential in sustaining long term, value-based partnerships with high-potential customers.

"A winning executive creates the conditions of victory before taking any initiative. A losing executive takes initiative before knowing how to succeed".
—Donald Krause, *The Art of War for Executives*

---

1. The Business Consultant

The strategic role of the Business Consultant is to demonstrate a detailed understanding of each high-potential customer's business and marketplace situation and how they define success for themselves.

By researching the customer's external and internal business situation, the Business Consultant will gather important intelligence about the current and future opportunities, as well as threats the customer will need to confront in order to succeed.

This level of insight provides the Sales Strategist with not only a clear view of each customer's strategic business situation, but also the opportunity to create the most appropriate business solutions.

2. The Relationship Manager

The Relationship Manager's primary role is to identify those individuals who either control or significantly influence the customer's strategic decision-making process, and to orchestrate effective relationships with them.

The Relationship Manager also focuses on pinpointing any other individuals who can provide additional intelligence, to validate and expand on the initial information the

Business Consultant has discovered about each customer's strategic situation.

3. The Competitor Analyst

In order to be successful, the Sales Strategist will need to implement carefully crafted sales strategies that outmanoeuvre competitors and create competitive advantage through genuine differentiation.

This is where the Competitor Analyst's role is key. Successful sales strategies rely heavily on accurate, timely intelligence, especially competitive intelligence.

The Competitor Analyst's role will be to build on the work of both the Business Consultant and the Relationship Manager, with the primary objective of gaining valuable insights into each competitor's strengths and weaknesses.

4. The Solutions Provider

In order to develop an effective solution, the Sales Strategist will need to assimilate the strategic intelligence gathered by the Business Consultant, the Relationship Manager and the Competitor Analyst.

Using that intelligence, the Solutions Provider's role is to identify and select those capabilities of their organisation that will mitigate the threats and resolve the problems that obstruct a customer's route to success.

Those capabilities will need to be embedded into a solution that will be genuinely differentiated from its competitors, and will satisfy those individuals who control or significantly influence the customer's decision-making process.

CHAPTER FOUR

Pursuing Strategic Growth

"The miner who starts panning whenever he sees water doesn't find much gold. The successful miner first looks for evidence".
—Buck Blessing, *Selling the Big Ticket*

In the introduction we saw that McDonald, Rogers and Woodburn observed, "We see companies starting to build models of account attractiveness" *(Key Customers – How to Manage Them Profitably)*.

Prioritising a portfolio of customers and prospects has always been an important part of every salesperson's work. Sometimes that account prioritisation is a formalised process. However, I have frequently found it is simply an intuitive process carried out almost exclusively in the mind of the salesperson and shared with very few others.

Even when the process is more formalised, it tends to focus almost exclusively on the more immediate or shorter-term potential of a customer – i.e., the business already closed in a current sales period, in addition to opportunities in the sales pipeline, usually covering a time frame of the next three to six months.

Using this shorter-term form of account prioritisation is popular because it is relatively easy to implement, and because it usually has that all-important "hard number" attached to the probable sales from each customer. This "hard" number frequently provides comfort to salespeople and sales managers when the need arises to justify how and where time and sales effort are being invested.

This shorter-term view, of course, does play a key part in the assessment of the potential and the importance of customers and prospects. However, if this shorter-term view becomes the *only* basis for assessment, it is going to produce an extremely myopic view of the sales potential across any customer portfolio.

This extremely restrictive view will only serve to inhibit the salesperson's ability to formulate medium- and longer-term business development strategies. Having well-developed strategies is essential in driving those longer-term, value-based partnerships and longer-term sales growth.

Looking for Oil

We said earlier that a change of perspective and attitude on the part of the salesperson is needed if we are to become more strategic. Without this change, we will be unable to sustain longer-term value to our customers and expand the range of our sales pipeline.

In order to initiate a successful strategic approach, we need to make a far more effective analysis of the longer-term potential of our customers and prospects. The process of prioritising a portfolio of customers needs to consider two major sales factors:

1. The first factor is "growth availability". This first step is an assessment of the customer's business profile with a

focus on *identifying* sales growth potential.

2. The second factor is "ease of accessibility". Here the focus is on *accessing* the strategic growth potential without inordinate difficulty or excessive cost.

In 2005, I was asked to lead a number of global workshops for an international oil field services company. Its sales teams were regularly bidding to win large oil exploration projects with major oil companies. Fascinated by the whole concept of oil exploration, I asked one of the senior engineers how they went about looking for new sources of oil.

Fortunately for me, he skipped over the complex technicalities and explained, "Basically, there a number of criteria we use that together point to the most likely location of oil. Then, using software and other processes, we carry out test drills where those criteria are most prevalent".

I asked him whether this approach actually guaranteed that there would be oil when they actually drilled. "Oh, no", he replied. "It's not a 100 percent certainty that we will find oil. What it does do, though, is reduce the time and the number of expensive test drillings that we need to carry out that eventually lead us to finding oil".

It struck me that this oil exploration process has some real similarities to the approach that the Sales Strategist needs to take. Locating growth potential is identifying where viable value-based partnerships will also mean that our longer-term sales opportunity pipeline is full.

Common Portfolio Issues

Before we move on to the actual prioritisation process, we need to review two customer portfolio issues that I run into on a fairly regular basis.

I was asked to conduct a number of seminars on strategic selling for a global technology company. During the seminar with the South African sales teams, one of the key account managers expressed a little scepticism about the need for any kind of prioritisation exercise. He was responsible for just three customers, but they were three of South Africa's biggest banks. He said, "They are all important!" and of course he was right.

With this kind of customer portfolio, there needs to be an initial exercise that first uncovers and then prioritises the underlying structure of what are really multipart organisations. A useful way forward is to view these kinds of organisations as a single macro marketplace, but made up of a number of differing types of micro businesses. Michael Porter describes these micro businesses, in his book *Competition in Global Industries,* as Business Units and Service Units.

Business Units operate as separate businesses under the umbrella of the overall organisation. They each offer specific products and services to specific customers and usually have specific competitors. Each Business Unit's performance is usually measured differently as well.

Typical Business Units in a banking organisation, for example, would be Retail Banking, Corporate Finance, Private Banking, Credit Cards and Asset Finance.

Service Units are internal departments like IT, Marketing, Human Resources, Finance and Facilities. Interestingly, they have customers too – the Business Units, to which they provide specific services and expertise. They also have competitors, like outsourcers.

At the other end of the portfolio spectrum, we have salespeople with a much larger portfolio of customers and prospects. I've encountered some portfolios of 70 customers and more. In this case, the reasoning against prioritisation is that there are simply too many accounts to make segmentation a viable exercise.

I've found that more and more organisations are viewing this size of portfolio for field-based salespeople as totally impractical. One client described the sales approach used to cover this size of portfolio as the "spray and pray" sales approach! In other words, it is a sales approach which, in my view, is both inefficient and ineffective.

Some organisations have reorganised their coverage strategy by establishing well-trained desk-based account managers to take care of the small to medium-size customers, leaving the field-based account managers focused on those organisations with the higher sales potential.

My recommendation is that the portfolio for field-based account managers be not higher than 20 customers and prospects. Covering more than that will significantly dilute sales effort and ultimately have a negative impact on sales productivity.

"Nothing appeals equally to all clients – or prospects. You need to research (and confirm) which individual clients will benefit most from your planned initiative".
—David H. Maister, *True Professionalism*

Let the Drilling Begin!

We are going to use a structured process to carry out our analysis. We will apply a range of relevant criteria to each customer's individual situation. The insight that this exercise provides will give us a clearer indication of where business development opportunities exist.

Similar to the oil exploration process, the search is not just for a few "barrels" of business development "oil" today. The Sales Strategist needs to see an attractive return on the investment of time and effort in the form of a consistent flow of new business over the longer term. It is with these kinds of customers that the development of value-based partnerships starts to make business sense.

I describe the process we are going to use to achieve customer prioritisation as "placing known criteria over an unknown situation". Similar to the oil exploration example, we will use relevant known criteria to help us look into the unknown world of the future growth potential across a portfolio of customers.

Some of the criteria could be called a "blinding flash of the obvious". However, in analysing and assessing even the most obvious criteria, we'll consequently be able to make better decisions about where to focus our time and effort.

We are going to assess individual customers and prospects from two perspectives: "Availability" and "Accessibility".

"Availability": Does this customer's strategic situation represent realistic growth opportunities?

"Accessibility": Can the growth opportunities be accessed without inordinate difficulty or excessive cost?

We will apply each criterion, in turn, in the form of a question. The response to each question will be "Yes", "No" or "Don't know". "Yes" will signify a positive response to the question based on accurate information we possess about the customer's situation, while "No" will signify a negative response. "Don't know" will indicate that we possess incomplete information about that particular criterion.

To get the very best from the exercise, choose a customer that you have already designated for business development. The exercise will provide you with some "real time" validation about your choice.

Remember, absolute honesty in your responses is paramount, or the principle of "garbage in, garbage out" will apply!

We will start with criteria that focus on the *availability* of potential future revenue:

APPLY THE PLAYBOOK – 1

Availability of Potential Future Revenue

Where is growth to be found?

Has your customer discussed and clarified their strategic business goals and key objectives with you?

Has your customer confirmed that business growth is one of their key objectives?

Are the current trends in the customer's key market sector(s) positive?

Is the customer a market leader whose reputation other organisations respect?

Is the customer's overall financial status in a healthy state?

Has the customer identified any major challenges that stand in the way of achieving their goal and objectives?

Can you identify early opportunities for your business solutions?

Have you validated the accuracy of your responses above with at least three key individuals across the customer's organisation?

What are the usual outcomes that we see from this first strategic step?

- The need to repeat the exercise and be a lot more honest!
- If we do apply more honesty the second time around, there may well be a level of concern about the number of "Don't knows".

- We may also want to scrutinise our positive responses more effectively.

The usual concern, though, at this first stage is a noticeable degree of frustration. Why? Because we cannot make a sound assessment of growth potential, due to a lack of intelligence in the form of missing, incomplete or unconfirmed information.

I was asked by a market leader in the printing and publishing sector to conduct a series of workshops for their European account teams. The objective of the workshops was the creation of strategically focused client relationship plans for their top-tier clients. At the conclusion of the three-day session, I sent the group away for a month to fine-tune their draft plans. They returned a month later for a one-day session in which to present their "polished" plans to a group of their executives.

The evening before the presentations, I was having dinner with one of the account managers and I asked him about his key learnings from the original three-day session. His response was so insightful that it has remained with me ever since.

He said, "When I came into the workshop, I knew what I knew but I didn't know what I didn't know! When I left the workshop I was clear about what I knew that was actually important and I was very clear about what I didn't know!"

He didn't see his sales situation as being in any way a negative one. His attitude was extremely positive, because he was now much clearer about the information he was missing. He saw that gathering that missing or incomplete information would provide him with the necessary strategic insight to move forward with his key customers.

Like this account manager, we have to see these kinds of "information gaps" as a necessary part of the strategic sales planning process. These holes enable us to see where we have to put into motion action plans that will make our route forward much clearer.

This exercise is much more than just simple information gathering. Like the pieces of a puzzle, a unique picture starts to form, of the partnering and business development environment for each individual customer.

Eventually we can build a strategic picture of sales potential across our complete account portfolio. We need to remember, though, that like a camera lens, that strategic picture needs to be reviewed and refocused regularly to keep pace with the inevitable changes that will constantly occur to the growth potential landscape of each customer.

I came across a Facebook page recently entitled, "Whoever said 'What you don't know can't hurt you' is a moron". Whilst I may have chosen slightly different words to express my feelings, I have to say that I agree completely with the overall sentiment!

When we focus on gathering the right intelligence about our marketplace, then the "strategic" picture takes on real shape and content.

"Information means getting facts – timely, accurate facts about the reality of conditions and circumstances in the competitive situation. Nothing in competition is more important than obtaining facts".
—Donald Krause, *The Art of War for Executives*

So if we have located some evidence of 'oil' we now need to know if we can actually retrieve it without inordinate difficulty and cost.

Let's move on to the second stage of our assessment and apply some criteria that focus on gaining insight into the *accessibility* of potential future revenue. We'll use the same "Yes", "No" and "Don't know" process as we did in the first stage.

APPLY THE PLAYBOOK – 2

Accessibility of Potential Future Revenue

Can you access the growth potential?

Do you have an installed base of products and services?

Do you have access to and credible relationships with the customer's strategic decision-makers and influencers?

Does your range of business solutions align with the customer's future business plans and key objectives?

Do you have validated evidence that the customer's current level of satisfaction with your organisation is positive?

Do recent SWOT analyses on each of your key competitors confirm that you have sufficient competitive advantage?

Do you have sufficient resources to create and develop additional new business over the medium and longer term?

Have you validated the accuracy of your responses above with key personnel in your own organisation?

What usual outcomes do we normally see from this second strategic step?

- The need to repeat the exercise and be a lot more honest!
- If we do apply more honesty the second time around, there may well be a level of concern about the number of "Don't know"s.
- We may also want to scrutinise our positive responses more effectively.

Sound familiar? The issues are very much the same as at the first stage. However, the primary issue at the second stage tends to be the same one time and time again. It's over-optimism by salespeople about the overall quality of their relationships with customers.

"Selling companies beware; there is a clear tendency for suppliers to be overoptimistic in their assessment of the relationship...buyers do not rate relationships in quite such a positive light. A relationship is actually at the stage of the least positive partner".
—McDonald and Woodburn, "Key Account Management", *London Financial Times*

Seeing Our Blind Spots

There are some real challenges in completing these two strategic assessments of growth potential. Any missing or incomplete information will pinpoint very precisely where we have to think about making serious changes in our sales behaviour.

If we want to start upgrading our sales approach to that of a Sales Strategist, we should now have some clear early evidence of where that upgrade should focus. We need to work on those areas where missing or incomplete information makes it difficult to come to any real conclusion about the growth potential status of our customer portfolio. These are strategic "blind spots" and show where we are operating "in the dark" and are most vulnerable to our competitors.

APPLY THE PLAYBOOK – 3

Selecting My High-Potential Customers

Using the "Availability" and "Accessibility" questions, first assess six of your customers/prospects that you believe are worthy of some business development activity.

Now review each of the assessments and decide on four or five actions for each customer, to either retrieve missing information or to confirm *with evidence* the positive responses.

Set a deadline of no more than 30 days to complete all the actions.

Once all the actions are completed, review the six customers/prospects again.

Decide which three customers reflect the most positive indicators of a potential value-based partnership.

Keep those three customers/prospects at the forefront of your mind as we move through the rest of this book.

Taking the time to assess your portfolio of customers and prospects using the structure we have reviewed in this chapter will create a real opportunity for personal progress, because you can:

- Continuously analyse your portfolio of customers, focusing on growth potential, not just on current business levels
- Look at your customers and prospects from a market perspective and from their point of view
- Manage your time and other resources more efficiently by focusing on high-potential customers

• Start to build value-based partnerships by becoming
  more strategic

Fail to Plan...

Identifying high-potential customers and prospects is a
critically important first step in becoming more strategic.
However, our analyses need to be seen as a "snapshot" taken
of a dynamic and changing marketplace.

Over time, change will certainly continue to impact
the whole account portfolio. You'll of course need to
perform ongoing reviews, so that any new issues that have
surfaced can be considered and factored into your customer
development strategies.

There are also time management issues that I will raise
here – because the most common excuse for not reserving
time for this vitally important prioritisation process is: "I
don't have enough time!"

"Fail to plan and you are planning to fail". I know some
see this as a cliché, but it's the truth.

Spending far too much time with customers and
prospects when there is no real sales-related justification
"steals" your time. These visits, often referred to as "courtesy
calls", frequently have no recognisable sales purpose or
objective.

In this new, challenging sales environment, these kinds
of meetings need to be shown the "Exit" door and quickly!

CHAPTER FIVE

The Business Consultant

"One thing we've discovered with certainty is that anything we do that makes the customer more successful inevitably results in a financial return for us".
—Jack Welch with Suzy Welch, *Winning*

Now that the Sales Strategist has a clearer view of where the "oil" might be located, the next step is to research, explore and "drill down" into each high-potential customer's business world – the oil field!

It is here that the Business Consultant's role really makes a pivotal contribution, if our intention is to work towards a value-based partnership with as many of our high-potential customers as possible.

Understanding each customer's strategic business situation and how they define success for themselves now has to become the focus of attention.

So what is it that we need to know as strategic Business Consultants?

There are three essential areas of insight that we need

to research and understand:

1. The customer's longer-term goal – their vision of future success
2. The customer's shorter-to-medium-term objectives – the key milestones that signpost the route to their longer-term goal
3. The customer's current and future opportunities and threats – the current and emerging challenges to the achievement of both the shorter-term objectives and the longer-term goal.

Do Your Homework

"The growing disconnect between what the buyer wants and what the sales rep provides contributes to the systematic failure of providing real added value to the customer".
—Qvidian's 2015 State of Sales Execution Report

Research and information gathering now become even more important in building a longer-term view of a customer's business environment.

The gathering of information has become a lot easier in the technology revolution. We are living in the era that has been dubbed "The Information Age".

Technological changes have brought dramatic new options in information gathering for salespeople. For the past couple of decades, new forms of commerce, research and communication have become commonplace in most parts of the world. The driving force behind much of this change is, of course, the Internet.

To point us in the right direction, here are a range of Internet-based and other sources of information that you can use to help to build a clearer picture of your customer's business environment:

- Customer's annual report ✓
- Chairman's statement ✓
- Customer's PR events and press releases ✓
- Customer's website ✓
- Customer's personnel
- Your own in-house subject matter experts
- Your business partners
- Analysts' reports: Factiva, Business Research, Experian ✓
- Media/trade press ✓
- YouTube ✓
- Social networks: Twitter, LinkedIn, Facebook ✓
  (✓ – probably/definitely available via the Internet)

So where should the Business Consultant start?

The Mission Statement

A customer's mission statement is a very good place to start, because it should state the corporate purpose and focus of each high-potential customer.

According to Dr. Chris Bart, one the world's leading researchers on organizational mission statements, a commercial mission statement should consist of three essential components.

---

1. Key market: Who is your customer's targeted client or customer population?
2. Contribution: What product or service do they provide to that customer population?
3. Distinction: What makes their products or services unique, so that their customers would choose them over other suppliers?
—"Industrial Firms and the Power of Mission", Industrial Marketing Management

---

The mission statement provides us with an excellent sense of the customer's basic raison d'être. Taking time to identify each of the three strategic components for your top customers is an extremely useful scene-setting exercise.

However, we also need to understand the actual environment in which the customer carries out their mission statement. We need clarity about how they conduct their day-to-day business and how their business strategies are applied to achieve their ultimate success.

The insight we gain from that level of research will also provide us with corroboration of the specific opportunities our initial growth potential analysis indicated. If our growth assessment is accurate, we should begin to see evidence of strategic "value-based partnering" opportunities starting to emerge from our research.

However, a word of caution here: we must remain strategic, because that "clearer" picture of the customer's world needs to be an outlook that stretches further than just the next few months.

The Longer-Term Goal – A Vision of Strategic Success

In simple terms, the goal of an organisation is its definition of longer-term success, sometimes described as its "preferred future". The time frame set for accomplishing a corporate goal can vary, but is usually around two to three years.

Well defined goals will consist of a fairly concise statement that will describe the status of the organisation at the end of the specified time frame.

"A goal is a statement of a desired future an organization wishes to achieve. It describes what the organization is trying to accomplish".
—Cothran and Wysocki, University of Florida

Goal statements will typically focus on any number of "desired futures", such as:

- Their competitive position – "become the undisputed market leader"
- Their market coverage – "become an established global business"
- Their range of products/services – "become an end-to-end solution provider"
- Their customer service – "become the recognised supplier of choice"

To be strategic, we need to capture the customer's goal – for when we establish the customer's longer-term definition of success, we gain early insight into where we can contribute longer-term strategic value.

APPLY THE PLAYBOOK – 4

My high-potential customers' strategic goals

Focus only on the three customers you have selected.

Do you know the longer-term goal of each high-potential customer?

Have you confirmed with key individuals in each organisation that their goal plays an integral and active part in their business strategy?

If you are clear about your customer's goal, what initial opportunity can you see to contribute strategic value?

If not, which information sources will you use to gain a clearer understanding of each customer's strategic goal?

→

What relevant case studies or testimonials can demonstrate your organisation's track record in enabling other customers to achieve these kinds of goals?

The Short- to Medium-Term Objectives – The Key Milestones

"Business objectives are the stated, measurable targets
of how to achieve business goals".
—Jim Riley, tutor2u

To realise its vision, an organisation will set itself a number of short-to-medium-term objectives that it needs to accomplish. These objectives act as milestones and enable the organisation to make and measure progress towards its goal, step by step.

Objectives are more specific than goal statements. The well-known "SMART" approach is commonly used by organisations to develop and communicate corporate objectives:

> Specific: A description that defines the focus of the objective
> Measurable: The quantifiable benchmarks that will be used to measure success
> Attainable: The resources needed to achieve the objective
> Relevant: The connection between the objective and the achievement of the goal
> Time-bound: The timescale for achieving the objective

Let's see how that might look.

In this example, the customer's goal is "to be recognised as the undisputed leader in the regional newspaper market by the end of 2018".

One of the important supporting SMART objectives might be:

"A major step towards becoming market leader in the regional newspaper market will be to increase circulation from 150,000 to 200,000 readers per week by 31 December 2017, through the creation of 75 additional retail distribution points".

Keep Your Eye on the Ball

There will a number of key objectives set by an organisation in support of its longer-term goal. As certain milestones are successfully reached, they will be replaced by new objectives which mark the next series of steps towards the ultimate goal.

When I was a key account manager, I won an extremely important sales opportunity with a major UK retailer – part of my client's longer-term project to completely re-engineer their business brand, structure and image. The retail sector was a development target for my company (which had no presence at all in the retail market), so my success was of strategic importance and I was duly recognised for my success.

However, just as the soccer team is at its most vulnerable when it has just scored, I "took my eye off the ball" and while my celebrations were in full flow, the customer moved on to the next stage of its strategy. By the time I reconnected with the key individuals, another supplier had moved in and I was left with just the memory of what might have been.

There is a real cost to being transactional and not strategic!

I should have taken the time to research and gain strategic insight into the customer's goal and the supporting objectives. If I had done that, I would have developed an understanding of the customer's strategic vision of success and the road map that had been set for its achievement. My lack of strategic vision meant that I missed both the current sale, and the potential sales opportunities that would have eventually emerged.

On another occasion, I was running a three-day strategic selling workshop for an international technology company. At the close of the first day's session, one of the account managers asked me if we could spare one hour of the following day for a presentation by one of his national government clients. The account manager and his team were engaged in a very important project to automate some key processes of the country's justice system. The presentation was going to be made by a senior government official who was also the project leader.

The following day, we briefly halted the workshop and, joined by a number of my client's senior management, the presentation proceeded. The project leader made a very engaging presentation which he brought towards a conclusion with a Q and A session.

He finally concluded his presentation with a closing statement which he directed to everybody in the room, "In concluding, I have a few words of advice for you all. It would help me considerably if when you visit me for a meeting, you could spend far less time talking about your plans, your products and your services and significantly more time talking about *my* plans and *my* products and *my* services!"

If anybody in the room had any lingering doubts about the need to pay close attention to the customer's priorities, they were dispelled very quickly!

Was Your Growth Potential Analysis Accurate?

There is also another important benefit from clarifying the customer's objectives as quickly as possible. The clarification process plays an important role in validating our original growth potential assessment. The customer's objectives will tell us quite quickly and clearly whether our initial assessment was really accurate or simply wishful thinking!

If we discover from our initial "drilling" activities that there is simply little or no business development "oil" after all, there are some important decisions we need make about the "opportunity cost".

What is "opportunity cost"? The New Oxford American Dictionary defines it as "the loss of potential gain from other alternatives when one alternative is chosen".

We will have to answer some important questions about our continuing investment of sales resources when the growth potential of a particular customer turns out to be less than we thought:

- What return on investment do we realistically need to achieve that will justify us spending more time and effort with this particular customer?
- If we do decide to maintain focus on this particular customer, what will we be sacrificing in growth opportunities elsewhere?

We also need to pay attention to how corporate objectives are cascaded downwards and translated into the objectives of each of the organisation's business and service units. These cascaded objectives must be tracked especially with the strategically important business and service units.

For example, what contribution are the key business units and the supporting service units like IT, Marketing, Human Resources or Finance expected to make if the overall organisational goal is to be achieved? What key objectives do they have that link to the overall vision?

This additional piece of research is invaluable, as it will confirm for us those business and service units which are more pivotal to the organisation's strategic success. It enables us to make far better decisions about where to apply our sales resources to greatest effect.

APPLY THE PLAYBOOK – 5

My Customers' Key Objectives

Review your three selected customers.

Using the SMART process, describe each customer's shorter-term objectives that are connected to the achievement of their longer-term goals.

From the insight you have now gained, which business and service units have a higher level of strategic importance in accomplishing each customer's goal?

Using SMART, describe the objectives of those strategically important business and service units.

Which units could provide current and future sales opportunities for you?

What testimonials do you have that prove your organisation provides business solutions that can help to achieve these kinds of objectives?

Identifying a customer's goal and the supporting objectives provides the Business Consultant with some real clarity of how each high-potential customer defines its pathway to success and what it needs to do to accomplish that success.

Although we are still at a relatively high level of insight, we can start to develop our value-based partnership plans. Those plans have to be developed around our ability to make a genuine contribution to the customer's ultimate success. It's right here that we have to start figuring out if we can deliver longer-term value to the customer, and if so, how we are going to make that happen.

Road Blocks on the Road to Success

There is one more level of insight that the Business Consultant needs to develop and factor into the planning process: to identify the threats and challenges the customer will encounter on their journey towards their goal.

Anticipating these potential obstacles will provide us with another great opportunity to demonstrate our strategic partnering credentials to the customer. There is also the distinct probability that more sales opportunities will come our way if we can provide the customer with solutions for overcoming these shorter-term obstacles.

A managing partner of a consulting firm I worked for described the kind of thinking needed to research these kinds of "roadblocks to progress" for the customer. The way salespeople approached this particular business development activity, he proposed, resulted in some very different levels of sales performance.

He said, "Average salespeople only look for a customer's needs – and of course, they will always find them. There are plenty of needs in every business, but that does not mean they are going to be selected as a priority item for action".

You will always find customer personnel that complain about a multitude of things that need to change. But for the most part, these needs are perceived as small irritations that require the occasional "corporate scratch" and not much more! A lot of sales time is wasted right here. This managing partner called these sales situations "phantom opportunities".

"Above-average salespeople are different", he said. "They look for issues. Issues are the needs that have begun to find their way onto the meeting agendas of managers and maybe even some executives. They have started to cause a business 'headache'.

"Most issues will need more formal discussion before any real action is taken. There is, however, almost always a short-term opportunity among the issues, so it's not a complete waste of time focusing on issues!"

In his view, great salespeople are different because they look for "trouble". From their strategic understanding of the customer's business, they are in a great position to anticipate, among the many needs and issues, those that are going to cause a real mission-critical problem for the customer.

The kinds of customer challenges we need to locate fall into two main categories:

- External market forces over which the customer has little or no control
- Internal organisational factors over which the customer does have control

External Market Forces

External market forces are business-related challenges that continuously emerge from *the customer's own marketplace* and compel them to review and modify their strategic plans in some way. These inevitable modifications frequently cause the customer to look for assistance externally, to keep their business strategies moving forward.

With research, the Business Consultant can identify these external market forces that will pose a threat to the customer's business strategy. I cannot stress enough the level of credibility a salesperson creates in the mind of a customer as the result of demonstrating this degree of insight. This insight also produces another significant benefit: the creation of a knowledge base from which the Sales Strategist can be proactive.

As we have already seen, transactional salespeople tend to be reactive and usually engage with the customer after many of the major buying decisions have already been made. The Sales Strategist seeks to engage with the customer earlier, when there is a much better opportunity to not only influence and shape the customer's requirements but also to create a significant degree of competitive advantage.

Here's a great example of how one account manager took the initiative with his customer and gained significant advantage as a result.

I was working with an international logistics organisation at their headquarters in Germany and one of the key account managers from Central America demonstrated how a strategic understanding of a specific marketplace led him to be able to deliver significant business value to a key customer. This level of insight also had the effect of creating clear differentiation between him and his more "transactional" competitors.

The account manager had made it his business to keep up to date on his government's import and export regulations. He had noticed in the financial press that one political commentator had highlighted an impending change in import laws that would have a profound effect on this particular customer's financial position. He made it his business to bring this imminent change to the attention of the CEO, who was not at all aware of the forthcoming change or of its potential impact on his business, even though his organisation had regular dealings with other logistics suppliers.

The account manager and the CEO were able to review the new legislation, make the necessary changes to the logistics processes and avert a looming crisis. The changes they made saved the customer a considerable amount of time, inconvenience and money. As you can imagine, the account manager's relationship with the CEO became significantly stronger, as did his competitive advantage.

"Being good at business development involves nothing more than a sincere interest in clients and their problems, and a willingness to go out and spend the time being helpful to them".
—David H. Maister, *True Professionalism*

The sources of information listed earlier in the chapter provide a lot of the core data needed to identify those potential challenges that your key customers will confront as they strive to achieve business success.

The PESTLE Effect

A popular way to help structure research of these external market forces is known as the PESTLE process. "PESTLE" represents six main factors that will impact every customer's business periodically, whether positively or negatively.

The six external factors are:

A **Political** factor is one which relates to the overall political environment and the attitudes of any major political parties, groups or movements. A typical research question could be: "How will the attitudes and policies of the current government and any major political parties or groups influence our customer's business strategy?"

An **Economic** factor is one which relates to the wider economy and usually includes levels of employment, costs of raw materials such as energy, interest rates and exchange and inflation rates. A typical research question here could be: "How might current and emerging economic trends affect the financial viability of the customer's business strategy?"

A **Sociological** factor is one which relates to the culture of the society within which an organization operates. It may include demographics, quality of education, distribution of wealth and any significant lifestyle trends. A typical research question here could be: "Which current and evolving social trends will have an impact on the customer's current business strategy?"

A **Technological** factor is one which relates to new inventions and development: for example, changes in information and mobile technology, e-commerce and new hi-tech manufacturing and logistics processes. A typical research question here could be: "How will new and emerging technologies shape the customer's business operations and its 'go-to- market' supply chain?"

A **Legal** factor is one which relates to national and regional laws, international trade regulations, monopolies and mergers' rules and consumer protection. A typical research question here could be: "How will compliance with new and emerging laws and regulations impact the customer's business strategy and its operations?"

An **Environmental** factor is one which relates to issues such as natural resources, waste disposal and recycling procedures. A typical research question would be: "How might ecological issues affect the customer's strategy and business operations?"

Let's take these insights and apply them to the three high-potential customers and prospects you have selected.

APPLY THE PLAYBOOK – 6

External Factors and Challenges

Review your three selected customers.

Using the PESTLE approach, identify those external market factors *currently* impacting your three selected customers.

Identify any additional external factors where the impact on the customer will be over *the medium/longer term.*

Which external factors will provide the most significant challenges?

Which business and service units will be affected the most?

Where can you identify current or emerging opportunities for your products and services?

→

> What testimonials do you have that demonstrate your organisation's track record in dealing with these kinds of challenges?

Internal Organisational Factors

Internal organisational factors are business-related "pressures" that emerge from *inside the customer's own organisation*. These internal pressures frequently cause the customer to upgrade their internal systems, processes and skills in order to improve their efficiency and effectiveness.

These upgrading initiatives can be connected to the external PESTLE factors we have just reviewed. However, they may indicate that the customer has simply identified organisational improvements that have to be made if their business strategy is to remain on course for success.

These kinds of internally generated initiatives provide a very valuable partnering opportunity for the Sales Strategist. Value-based partnerships will be strengthened and competitive advantage increased when you can provide the customer with the expertise that contributes to the success of these initiatives.

So what are the kinds of projects and programmes for which we are looking? The Business Consultant knows that further research is vital in uncovering these kinds of current and emerging customer initiatives. We will apply a similar approach to the one we used to identify the external market forces; this time we will use the structure "SPIESO" to highlight those internal factors that will point towards a possible "upgrade" initiative.

Here are some examples of SPIESO in action:

Solutions relate to the customer's range of products and services.

Is the customer planning to launch new products and services? Seeking to improve product and service quality?

Adding greater value through strategic alliances?

Performance relates to the customer's business effectiveness and efficiency.

Is the customer focused on reducing operating expenses? Looking to improve cash flow? Needing to protect margins?

Image relates to the customer's status and position in its market.

Is the customer currently relaunching its brand? Targeting market leadership? Moving upmarket?

Employees relates to the customer's personnel.

Is the customer aiming to reduce staff turnover? Upgrading its training and development curriculum? Wanting to improve morale?

Sales relates to the customer's trading performance in its marketplace.

Is the customer seeking to improve its competitive advantage? Creating greater differentiation? Neutralising a key competitor?

Operations relates to the customer's core business processes.

Is the customer attempting to reduce order processing time? Improving e-commerce systems? Streamlining administrative processes?

APPLY THE PLAYBOOK – 7

Internal Factors and Challenges

Review your three selected customers.

Using the SPIESO approach, identify any internal factors currently impacting your three selected customers.

Which internal pressures will provide the most significant challenges?

$\rightarrow$

Which business and service units will be affected the most?

What current or emerging opportunities can you identify for your products and services?

What testimonials do you have that demonstrate your organisation's track record in providing business solutions that address these kinds of challenges?

The research calls for a significant investment of your time. However, there are profitable payoffs for the quality time and effort that you invest. Exploring and assessing these "internal" pressures will provide the strategic salesperson with even more opportunities to demonstrate their partnering credentials to the customer.

Equally important, this level of quality research invariably uncovers new sales opportunities that will always remain hidden from the transactional salesperson.

What You Don't Know Can Hurt You

So what do we know as this stage?

The Goal: a definition of what longer-term success means for the customer.

The Objectives: the series of measurable, shorter-term milestones that define the customer's progress towards its goal.

The Challenges: the external market pressures that create barriers and obstacles to the customer's attainment of its ultimate goal and the successful accomplishment of its key objectives.

The Initiatives: those programmes and projects that the customer will introduce to upgrade its effectiveness and efficiency, in order to achieve its goal, meet its objectives and overcome any obstacles and barriers to success.

As we have discussed, one of the Business Consultant's

most critical priorities is to gather and assess key information about the marketplace in which the Sales Strategist operates. The quality of information we have already gained about our high-potential customers provides us with a very effective first base of "intelligence" which we can use to create, apply and sustain our overall sales strategy.

"Information is the radar of strategy".
—Rick Page, *Hope Is Not a Strategy*

There are other factors which we will cover in the following chapters that we will need to consider if our sales strategy is to be developed effectively. Right now the task at hand is to assess and validate the basic research gathered so far about the customer's strategic business environment.

It is at this point that the role of the Relationship Manager begins to emerge as a mission-critical partner of the Business Consultant.

First, we need to identify the missing or incomplete "intelligence" that we still need to retrieve, and set the timeline for its retrieval. We also have to decide *who* can provide that intelligence. Our sales mantra at this stage needs to be "What you don't know CAN hurt you"! Research has to be validated, and with those individuals in the customer's business who are in the very best position to endorse our findings.

In my experience, salespeople can be frequently over-optimistic about their sales situation. So when we are verifying key information, triangulation is vitally important. Always select more than just one or two individuals to validate initial research. This is especially important if it is information around which we have developed key aspects of our sales strategy.

We also need to make sure these individuals are not lower-level customer personnel who, while potentially very helpful and supportive, may have a limited view of their own organisation's strategic situation.

A point worth remembering here is that in our quest to be Sales Strategists and focusing more on the medium- and longer-term view, we don't want to overlook what is under our very noses! That is why we have looked for current sales opportunities throughout the process of building our understanding of the customer's strategic business environment.

The Sales Strategist knows how to keep the balance between locating and developing emerging sales opportunities and pursuing and winning the opportunities that are already in play. After all, if we don't engage successfully in addressing the customer's shorter-term business challenges, there may not be a longer-term!

In order to keep our strategic balance, we have to develop a mind-set that sees things from the customer's perspective. Whatever opportunities appear on our sales radar, we need to qualify them by first asking these two important questions:

- How important to the customer's business strategy is the business issue we have identified as a sales opportunity for ourselves?
- Is it a need or an issue or is it "trouble"? Is it an irritation, a headache or something more terminal?

Quality Information = Quality Decisions

We have now covered the elements that create a fundamental understanding of the customer's strategic business environment. This level of clarity will enable us to make better decisions about how and where we can contribute unique business value to our customers. For those customers that have real growth potential, we will be able to see far more clearly where those longer-term, value-based customer partnerships can be developed.

These deeper insights into the customer's business environment have also started to reveal those previously hidden, current and longer-term sales opportunities. We can now see how this level of strategic insight can dramatically expand our sales pipeline and add a great deal more accuracy to future sales forecasting.

APPLY THE PLAYBOOK – 8

Your Strategic Position

Review your position with each of your three selected customers.

Is your initial assessment of the long-term value of each customer still valid?

How many current and potential sales opportunities have you identified?

What is the estimated value of those opportunities?

Which business and service units are now your priority targets?

Are you satisfied with your potential Return on Investment?

For each customer, which business and service units are your priority targets?

What actions do you need to take to retrieve missing or incomplete information?

Who will you meet with in order to validate and prioritise the intelligence you have gathered so far?

What are the most important questions you need to ask them?

CHAPTER SIX

The Relationship Manager

> "Every company has two organizational structures:
> The formal one is written on the charts; the other is the
> everyday relationship of the men and women in the
> organization".
> —Harold S. Geneen (former CEO, ITT), *Managing*

We know that high-quality intelligence is at the heart of effective sales plans and strategies, whether we are building a stronger, value-based customer relationship or pursuing a specific sales opportunity. The Sales Strategist is acutely aware that strategic intelligence has to be validated and probed deeply.

This clarification process is only truly effective when it is affirmed by those individuals that have strategic decision-making responsibilities, or at least with the "trusted lieutenants" who have strong, credible relationships with them.

This is where the role of the Relationship Manager becomes pivotal to strategic sales success and the forging of value-based partnerships. However, it is at this point that maintaining a strategic perspective is under most threat.

"It's Not What You Know But..."

When I ask even the most experienced sales professionals, "Who are the most important customer personnel with whom you need to develop an ongoing relationship?" the response will be very quick, loud and confident: "Decision makers and influencers, of course!"

Correct!

So where's the threat?

The threat lies with what actually happens in reality.

That reality is revealed by some enlightening research carried out by McGraw-Hill and included in *Key Customers – How to Manage Them Profitably* (McDonald, Rogers and Woodburn):

Number of employees in customer's business	Average number of buying influences (DMU)*	Average number of contacts made by salespeople
Under 200	3.42	1.72
201–400	4.85	1.75
401–1,000	5.81	1.90
Over 1,000	6.50	1.65

*Decision Making Unit

There are two sales issues revealed by this unique research that will need to be remedied if we are to stand any chance of becoming effective Sales Strategists and competing effectively in the post-recessionary sales environment.

1. The first, most obvious issue is that the "contacts" coverage for most salespeople is, on average, woefully inadequate.
2. The less obvious issue is that there is no evidence that the customer contacts made by salespeople have any role in the DMU.

The research provides a clear example of where the traditional, transactional customer relationship approach has to be upgraded as an immediate priority. We cannot be strategic if our customer relationship base is so appallingly narrow. This is the change in sales approach which, in my view, is the most important of all, if we want to make the move from less transactional to more strategic selling.

One of the quickest methods I have discovered to assess how much transactional selling is going on in any sales organisation is to identify at which levels of the customer's organisation salespeople have the majority of their active customer relationships.

Believe me: the McGraw-Hill research we looked at on the previous page is very accurate!

Breaking Out

In my experience, transactional salespeople have the majority of their relationships at the lower levels of a customer's organisation, and usually in one specific service unit. There is nothing inherently wrong with this level of relationship, provided it is not the *only* point in the customer's organisation where we have our important and active relationships.

Lower-level relationships, with employees at operational and supervisory levels, have a role to play and cannot be ignored. However, you will not uncover at these levels the mission-critical insights and intelligence or decision-making influences that you need in order to develop value-based partnerships.

One account manager, who realised that he needed to expand his customer relationships to become more strategic, bemoaned the fact that he had become "locked" into lower-level relationships. He described his dilemma as being "stuck like a fly on flypaper!"

If you have similar relationship issues, you will need to exercise great care and act very carefully when you start to expand your coverage and develop new relationships – or you may just turn friends into foes!

Another key issue for the Relationship Manager to consider is the availability of sales resources needed to initiate, build and sustain these higher-level management and executive-level relationships so pivotal to our longer-term success. These higher-level relationships demand a higher level of skill, resource and aptitude if they are to be effective.

The Sales Strategist will want to be absolutely confident that the individual relationship targeting is not only accurate but is also going to be effective.

To maintain a strategic perspective the Relationship Manager will need to answer three key questions:

1. In my high-potential customers' organisations, with which individuals do I need to regularly consult in order to gain, validate and maintain an accurate strategic perspective?
2. Which of these individuals is also an active member of the Decision Making Unit (DMU), either managing or influencing the strategic decision-making process?
3. Who in my own organisation will need to support me by taking responsibility for the development of some of these important relationships?

With Whom Should I Consult?

The answer to this important question will probably have started to emerge as the Business Consultant engaged in the strategic research we covered in Chapter Four.

Let's say that, in the Business Consultant's role, we have already engaged in initial strategic research of a high-potential customer. In the course of our research we have come across some useful information about the customer's goal, its objectives or maybe some of its external or internal business challenges.

The role of the Relationship Manager should now come into play. These early insights should start to point us towards some specific roles and functions that may be clearly affected by those same business issues.

At this point we can see how these two Sales Strategist roles, the Business Consultant and the Relationship Manager, need to start operating as a virtual partnership. As the one role gathers strategic intelligence, the other role applies that insight, to steer it towards the specific individuals we will need to contact.

Let's say that your customer's chairman has declared in their Annual Report to Shareholders that their goal is to become leader in a particular market sector within three years, and that e-commerce will play a key role in supporting that initiative. You could quickly deduce that there are probably some individuals in Sales, Marketing and IT who will be likely sources of more-specific intelligence about the achievement of that specific goal.

At first sight, the logical deduction we have made in this example looks to be embarrassingly simple. However, let's be perfectly clear that it only became simpler because we used a strategic perspective to focus our research. It is that research that has helped to guide our subsequent sales decisions to focus on certain customer personnel.

Remember our account executive in Chapter Three, who watched the YouTube video of his customer's annual shareholders meeting? He was able to gather vital intelligence from some key individuals without even scheduling an appointment with them!

A point to consider here is that the gathering of strategic information has something of a "What came first, the chicken or the egg?" quality to it. We need to get information fairly quickly, but we also need to make sure that the information is of the right quality. We don't want to waste a lot of time researching, analysing and trying to validate the wrong issues and going seriously off-piste!

To reduce the likelihood of this happening, Relationship Managers use "strategic shortcuts" to focus their research more effectively. These shortcuts in the sales research process help them identify key individuals and validate research more quickly.

At the information gathering stage, Relationship Managers connect with as many individuals as possible to develop an early view of the customer's strategic environment. Over time there will be a natural reduction in the number of individuals on whom we need to focus our relationship-building skills.

"Selling skills are paramount. It will also be important...
to gain an understanding of how the decision on
supplier selection will be made, who will influence the
decision and in what way, their modus operandi and their
personalities".
—McDonald, Rogers and Woodburn, *Key Customers –
How to Manage Them Profitably*

Here's a very good example of how one key account manager quickly and easily expanded her coverage of the customer's organisation.

I was working with a client in the retail sector, where the focus was on helping the key account team sell more strategically to their most important customers. One of the team had just taken over as a key account manager for one of the UK's major supermarket chains.

My client's past sales success with this customer was unimpressive and had fallen way below their targeted sales performance. The new account manager told me that she had just one active contact, a procurement manager based at her customer's headquarters. She added that whilst she saw the need for in-depth strategic research, she also saw that time was really against her and that it was essential to expand her coverage of the customer's organisation beyond the procurement department as quickly as possible.

So I told her how to take a shortcut with her research and leverage the one relationship she had. I suggested she approach her lone contact for help by asking a very simple question:

"Who else in your organisation do *you* think I should talk to?"

She said she would give it a try, and one month later when the whole team returned for a progress review, she greeted me with a smile and the words, "Boy, did you give me a high-class problem!" I was fascinated to find out what kind of "problem" I had given her.

When it came to her turn to tell us what progress she had made, she reminded me of the question I had suggested she ask her single contact. She said, "I asked him who else I should talk to in his organisation and he replied that he would give it some thought and let me know.

"When I got back to my office later that day, I saw he had sent me an email. When I opened the email it contained ten names of other people in the organisation he thought could help me!"

This very simple question has proved, time after time, to be an extremely useful "shortcut" in revealing how improved customer coverage can be generated quite quickly. It's a question that every Relationship Manager will ask consistently and regularly. However, remember asking the "shortcut" question does not mean that the strategic research we introduced earlier in this chapter becomes unnecessary. It means that we can focus our attention on the "right" people more quickly, in order to ensure that our intelligence is both accurate and relevant.

Are Your Bases Covered?

Asking this simple "shortcut" question is also a very effective way of cross-checking your coverage of key clients, even when you may think that you already have your relationship "bases" covered.

Here's a situation that illustrates the potential danger of being complacent and suddenly finding out that your "ducks" may not be quite as much "in a row" as you think!

I was working with a financial services sales team, and at the conclusion of the two-day workshop I asked each delegate to tell me three specific actions they would commit to implementing that they believed would have a positive and immediate impact on their sales effectiveness. As customer coverage was a topic that we had covered in some detail, asking the simple question, "Who else in your organisation do you think I should talk to?" appeared on the commitments of two or three of the salespeople in the group.

About two months later, the group reassembled to review their experiences in applying their commitments. We were listening to some really great feedback when we got to one of the more senior salespeople. He grabbed everybody's attention when he told us that one of his commitments had produced £6 million of business.

The single action that produced such a significant result was to ask each of his client contacts, over a four-week period, the simple question:

"Who else in your organisation do you think I should talk to?"

He told us of one particular client situation. He was sharing the business from this important client with another competitor. His half of the business was worth around £6 million per year.

He had tried several times to win all of the business, but was told by the CEO that because he wanted to keep both companies "on their toes", he had no immediate plans to give all of the business to one company. He then went on to tell us that he'd almost decided against asking the question of this client, since he enjoyed such an excellent relationship with the CEO. Why would you ask the question if you have a healthy relationship with the CEO?

However, he did decide to ask him the question and received an interesting response. The CEO told him that he might want to meet with one of his senior sales managers. He explained that he had given the sales manager a special project which involved a complete review of the organisation's "go-to-market" sales strategy. He had asked him to report back with ideas and recommendations that could improve the business's performance.

He went on to say that he had no idea what his sales manager was going to propose, but the presentation was scheduled to take place in a couple weeks.

The account manager made hasty arrangements to meet the sales manager, and at the meeting was shocked when he heard one of the key recommendations that the sales manager was going to make to the CEO: that all of the organisation's business should go to a single supplier, in order to leverage better pricing and service levels. The preferred single supplier was…his competitor!

Happily, though, he described how he was able to deal with the crisis by moving quickly and, with his sales director, preparing a counter-proposal that provided far better terms and conditions. As a result, they became the preferred supplier and the sales manager's recommendation was accepted by the CEO.

I'll leave you to work out what might have happened if he had decided *not* to ask the question: "Who else in your organisation do you think I should talk to?"

The" shortcut" question is one that every Relationship Manager will ask consistently and regularly. However, just asking the question does not mean that strategic research becomes unnecessary.

Relationship Managers know that the issues thrown up by the strategic research gathered by the Business Consultant provide and confirm the most accurate indicators of who should be on the "potential contacts" radar.

"The reason enlightened rulers and competent commanders win victories, achieve outstanding success and surpass ordinary people is that they know critical information in advance".
Sun Tzu – *Art of War*

Access and Credibility

The strategic research also informs the Business Consultant and the Relationship Manager of the specific customer intelligence that will need to be explored, validated and expanded in meetings with these key customer contacts. If quality strategic research is not available to us, then our chances of gaining access to these key individuals in the first place becomes highly unlikely. Failure to demonstrate any real insight of our customer's strategic situation will always work against us.

How can we define the purpose of the meeting to an extremely busy executive or senior manager when we have no basis for answering the inevitable "What's in it for me" question? Even if we do manage to set up a meeting with a key executive or manager, we still are in mortal danger.

The absence of strategic research means that we will almost certainly default to the more "transactional" theme in our customer meetings. We will find ourselves focused on promoting our company and its range of products and services rather than presenting compelling, customer-focused value propositions.

The belief that we can develop rapport and credibility with strategically oriented individuals using this kind of tactical, self-focused approach is a complete delusion. The delusion becomes all too obvious when we attempt to set up a second meeting with these very important people – it will not end well!

APPLY THE PLAYBOOK – 9

Key Individuals – My Relationships Status (1)

Review your individual relationship status with each of the three customers you have selected.

Based on the McGraw-Hill research, how many individuals do you believe are likely to be in the Decision Making Unit (DMU) for each of your three selected customers?

How many **active** individual relationships do you have with each of your selected customers?

How many **active** individual relationships do you have with each of the important business and service units?

How many are at the executive level? How many are at management level? How many are at the supervisory or operational level?

With which executives and senior managers do you need to arrange meetings?

Is the quality of your strategic research relevant and sufficient enough to provide a compelling reason for those executives or senior managers to spend time with you?

The Decision Making Unit (DMU)

The DMU is made up of two distinct types of individuals:

- Those individuals with the formal authority to make decisions on behalf of the customer
- Those individuals who are consulted with by the formal decision-makers for their professional advice and

personal opinions, in order that the most advantageous decision can be made

---

"A decision maker may have authority formally assigned but is expected to listen seriously to and reach agreement with a variety of staff experts, task forces, committees and other managers who have interests in the issues supposedly under the command of the decision maker".
—Cohen and Bradford, *Influence Without Authority*

The story that we reviewed earlier in this chapter provides us with a simple example of how these two distinct roles operate. The CEO made the final decision about which supplier would be given all of the business. The sales manager's report influenced the CEO about what that decision should be.

Both the CEO and the sales manager were in the DMU. What we don't know from the story are the identities of other individuals whose opinions the CEO might have also listened to prior to making his final decision. That additional information would be critical if the account manager had needed to know the composition of the whole DMU.

All contacts that we make in any customer's organisation have some value. However, some contacts are far more valuable than others, because of the quality of intelligence they possess and their role in the decision-making process.

So where do we start the process of narrowing down our group of contacts to those who are actually in the DMU?

Identifying the *formal* members of the DMU is probably easier than identifying the *informal* members. Formal members are those who have an organisationally approved role for making or approving the final strategic decisions.

Decision-makers will have the formal authority to commit their organisations to a specific direction, like "signing off" on a significant investment or the adoption of the strategic goal. They will also be directly involved in the endorsement of the various corporate objectives that will need to be achieved to arrive at that goal. The decision-making role will often carry over into how the organisational goal and objectives are devolved to the various business and service units.

Relationship Managers will focus on identifying these individuals as early as possible in the sales process, as they set the strategic direction of the organisation. They will also get to know how these decision-makers will benefit personally from the organisation's achievement of strategic success.

So how do you discover the identity of the decision-maker?

You could always ask!

The simplest route is frequently the best route. As the Business Consultant is retrieving the strategic business intelligence we covered in Chapter Three, the Relationship Manager should be ready to ask these kinds of questions:

"Who signed off the longer-term goal of the organisation?"

"Who decides which internal projects and programmes will be the priority initiatives?"

"Who makes the final decision about investment in our kinds of business solutions?"

Many salespeople are reluctant to ask these kinds of questions, believing that they are "too direct" or perceiving that customer personnel will react negatively to what they see as invasive.

Here's a great example of a situation when the simple route turned out to be the best route.

I was sitting in on two client meetings with a technology salesperson who was new to her role. One meeting was with the senior partner of a firm of architects, and the other meeting was with the IT manager at a private college.

Although she was new to her role, she did a great job managing both meetings confidently and competently. One thing she did particularly well at both meetings was to ask the simple question: "Who will make the final decision?"

In both cases she received a very clear and non-defensive response.

In the case of the senior partner, he told her who the decision-maker was and also explained the decision-making process without being prompted.

The IT manager at the private school told her the name of the decision-maker and then went on to say he was on the premises and immediately invited him to their meeting!

There may be occasional "push-back" to these kinds of questions; however, if you never ask you may never know who is controlling the strategic DMU. We need to be "professionally" persistent in asking these questions across a wide range of strategic contacts. The more individuals you ask, the quicker you will learn the identity of the most "likely suspect"!

Gaining Access

But what do you do when you know the identity of the decision-maker but cannot gain access to them?

Salespeople are frequently unsuccessful in setting up meetings with strategic decision-makers. These individuals are typically high-ranking executives or very senior managers with busy schedules. Trying to gain access to them by using a direct approach like a telephone call can be extremely frustrating.

According to Nicolas Read and Stephen Bistritz, in *Selling to the C-Suite,* the success rate in getting a meeting with an executive using the direct approach, like a telephone call, is around 20 percent. If a letter or email is sent in advance of the telephone call, the success rate rises to 25 percent. However, as the research shows, you are likely to be unsuccessful most of the time if you try to get a meeting with a strategic decision-maker using a direct approach.

You could, of course, try a different route. External referrals from connections in common on social media sites like LinkedIn have been used to arrange exccutive meetings when the direct approach has failed. Sometimes your business partners or trusted external consultants with access to these executives can help you set up meetings.

Read and Bistritz's research shows that this "indirect" route is successful around 44 percent of the time. Win one, lose one! It is still a relatively inefficient method, but is, on average, around twice as successful as the "direct" route.

However, there is another route to setting up meetings with executives that stands out way above the others in terms of success – the "supporter" approach.

This approach leverages *internal* referrals from your target executive's own organisation. Typical sources of internal referrals are the executive's own direct reports, peer executives in other business or service units or simply individuals that have a strong personal relationship with that executive.

Read and Bistritz's research shows that the "supporter" approach is successful 84 percent of the time in enabling a salesperson to arrange a meeting with a key executive or senior manager.

So What Is a Supporter?

A potential supporter is an internal or external individual who has credibility and influence with a formal decision-maker. These individuals will actively support us when they see that we are able to deliver business value to the organisation and personal value to them.

They are typically described in a number of ways – "mentors", "champions" or "sponsors" are just a few of their designations. Their support and influence is invaluable because they will "open executive doors" for you and some will also be active members of the strategic DMU.

So if access to the strategic "movers and shakers" can be best accomplished through a supporter, what makes a great supporter?

First we need to understand that the Business Consultant and the Relationship Manager have already made significant progress in identifying potential candidates. We now need to focus completely on the Relationship Manager's role in gathering further intelligence about these potential supporters that can help us gain access to the all-important decision-maker. We will also use this specific intelligence-gathering activity to understand the composition of the DMU.

Influence – Is It Like Trying to Catch the Wind?

We have already indicated that a critical characteristic of an effective supporter is that they have "influence". So what is "influence" and how can we identify it?

> "Influence is the ability to alter or sway an individual's or a group's thoughts, beliefs, or actions without the might of the formal hierarchical system to support that ability".
> —Veritas Rising International, Leadership Consultants

As we see from the definition above, one of the first principles we need to recognise is that one individual can "influence" another individual regardless of their formal position in an organisation. Direct reports influence their managers; managers influence executives; and external "experts" influence internal personnel.

Influence itself is somewhat intangible. Like the breeze on a windy day, you can feel and see its effect, but not its physical form.

Similarly, influence can be felt and seen, for example, by the way in which a lower-level individual's interaction with a senior executive is welcomed positively. At the same meeting, an interaction with a more-senior manager might be handled by the same executive in a much more detached and less respectful way.

Transactional salespeople are extremely naive about the role of informal influence, whilst Sales Strategists are extremely astute.

In my opinion, tracking and defining influence is one of the decisive factors in quickly distinguishing a strategic approach from a transactional approach. It is one of the main reasons Sales Strategists always outperform their sales targets, whilst transactional salespeople's performance frequently remains inconsistent and unreliable.

Sales Strategists know who will help them to win and not simply compete!

"Begin discreetly mapping the zones of influence from your first meeting with your client".
—Rick Page, *Hope Is Not a Strategy*

Here's a perfect example from my personal sales experience showing the price I paid for political naiveté.

I took a call from the secretary to the human resources director of a major international bank based in London. She was calling to advise me that a Request for Proposal (RFP) would be arriving on my desk in the next few days.

The HR director's previous company was a longstanding client in the US, where she also headed up human resources with another bank. She had been in her new role for about 12 months and wanted to put in place some new training and development initiatives to prepare staff for the "Big Bang" in financial services that took place in the UK in the mid-1980s.

Her secretary told me that the implementation schedule was "tight", so the RFP had been written using wording and terms taken directly from my company's products and services. She hoped that would help me respond quickly.

As you can imagine, I felt very confident that we were in a great position to win the business. She was a main board director and head of the project, she already had a very positive experience of our products and services in the US and the RFP was written using our language. Adding to my confidence, I was already doing some business in the investment management part of the bank with another executive sponsor.

I completed the proposal and very quickly received a response. She wanted to run three "pilot" programmes for a cross-section of her target audience and, provided the feedback was good, the programme would then be "rolled out" across the bank.

It was looking better all the time!

We ran the pilot programmes and the feedback was excellent. All I needed now was the order and we could get on with the main event.

So I waited...and waited...and waited. No call, no communication, no order. I tried telephoning but she was never able to take the call – in meetings, travelling, on vacation or simply "not here right now".

Somewhat perplexed and under pressure from my sales director because the business was in my sales forecast, I tried calling after hours and finally made contact. She apologised profusely for not returning my calls, saying she had been incredibly busy. I took a positive approach and reminded her of the success of the pilots, then said that I wanted to discuss the timetable for the roll-out across the bank, because my understanding was that the project was on a "tight" schedule.

She politely sidestepped my positive approach and said, "Terry, we really liked your proposal...".

Any experienced salesperson will know what came next. It was that fateful word "but".

"BUT...we have decided not to put all of our eggs in one basket".

I was in a state of some shock, as all of my ducks had appeared to be in a very orderly row. How could this happen? What had gone wrong?

She apologised but concluded by saying that I should continue my good work with investment management and maybe we would get another chance to work with her on a major project at some other time.

Here is a very good example of being totally beguiled by the formal components of a strategic sales situation. On the surface, everything could not have looked rosier. However, behind the scenes, informal influence was clearly playing a powerful role and my HR director, although on the main board, was clearly not as influential as I had imagined.

The decision-making process and the actual DMU were both completely unknown to me, and I suffered the ultimate consequence of my strategic ignorance and naïveté.

We have to fully embrace the need to identify the agendas of those individuals who possess the persuasive power of informal influence with decision-makers and on the decision-making process itself. This insight is vital if we are to define the composition of the DMU. If we do not focus sales resources on understanding its composition, then we are in danger of completely overlooking or even totally ignoring some very important people.

The impact of this state of affairs on our strategic plans could well be devastating. It will certainly not end well!

The Three Characteristics of Influencers

Influencers possess three specific characteristics that we need to recognize. The more of these characteristics that a single individual possesses, the more likely they are to be potentially important "influencers".

1. Expertise
Which individuals possess specialist knowledge and recognised expertise about the strategic issues with which we are concerned?

2. Track Record
Which individuals have a track record of success leading or working on similar strategic projects?

3. Personal Relationships
Which individuals have a close family, business or social relationship with the decision-maker?

Relationship Managers know that these characteristics will provide certain individuals with potential influence in the decision-making process. Their opinions and advice will be valued by the decision-makers, and it is therefore their support we will need to recruit and harness if we are going to make strategic progress.

Looking beyond the organisation's formal hierarchy is important.

Whilst we have to respect the customer's formal lines of authority, we will be in serious trouble if we believe that this is the sole source of decision-making influence. Here's an example of what I mean.

I was sitting in on a sales meeting with an account manager from a technology company, and the CIO and a colleague of his client, a firm of architects in the southwest UK.

We had already established before the meeting that the CIO was the decision-maker, so I was intrigued by the presence of a colleague, a young man in his early twenties. During the meeting, I noticed that the account manager was paying as much attention to the young man as he was to the CIO.

The meeting went well, and after the CIO and his young colleague had left the room, the account manager looked at me and asked me, with a slight smile on his face, "How do you think the meeting went?"

I replied that the meeting had gone well but I was quite curious about the attention he was paying to the young man, especially since the decision-maker was in the meeting.

He explained, "The CIO will make the final decision, but

his young direct report is the son of the managing director and still lives at home. I know that he will discuss our meeting with his father over dinner tonight and that he needs to recommend us as the preferred supplier. The CIO and I had discussed prior to the meeting that it was very important that we included him in the decision-making process".

The Pieces of the Influence Puzzle

Whilst the possession of any or all of these three characteristics provides a basis for potential influence, we still need to be able to identify some observable evidence that will point to its actual existence.

I was conducting a strategic workshop follow-up with some account managers from a global telecom supplier. One of the account managers told me that he had been working with his team in becoming more proficient at identifying customer personnel who had influence with decision-making executives.

He and his team had started to collate a number of "observable" behaviours that together highlighted those individuals that probably had influence with decision-makers, as well as those individuals that probably did not.

His point was that while some of the behaviours might appear insignificant, each piece of the puzzle was important when building a more visible picture of the oftentimes elusive identity of those individuals with influence.

These are some of the behaviours that he and his team were observing:

- Who was included in the circulation list of any formal meeting invitations that he and the team had organised where the decision-maker would be present?
- Were there surprising inclusions? Who were they and why were they attending?
- Who was not included and why?
- Were there unexpected attendees from other business

and service units? Why were they attending?
- Who were we expecting to attend that did not show up?
- Whose name was mentioned more than once by the decision-maker but was not in attendance?
- During the meeting, whose opinion was sought by the decision-maker? Whose opinion was not?
- Who offered advice that the decision-maker acknowledged positively? Who tried but was shut down or ignored by the decision-maker?
- What did the decision-maker's body language tell you about their positive or negative attitude to certain individuals?
- Who was on the circulation list for the minutes of these meetings?

"Knowing the concerns, objectives and styles of
the people you want to influence is fundamental
for determining what you will need to offer to gain
cooperation".
—Cohen and Bradford, *Influence Without Authority*

Sometimes account managers tell me that this degree of sales sophistication is unnecessary when you are dealing with small or medium-size customers. They tell me that tracking decision-makers, gathering information and identifying influence is fairly straightforward, because there's not much to know and there seem to be so few people involved in the decision-making process.

I always tell the account managers to ask their customer contacts the question that we focused on earlier, "Who else do you think I should speak to about this issue?" Invariably they report back that the response from their customer was "my accountant" or "my lawyer" or some other external expert or adviser.

Influence is not reserved exclusively for those individuals who are employees of the organisation. Opinions and advice that is valued by decision-makers originates from external sources as well.

So, having identified those individuals who have influence, how does the Relationship Manager convert that personal influence into personal support?

The first step will be to set up one-to-one meetings with each potential supporter as quickly as possible. Relationship Managers know the importance of understanding the personal objectives and preferences of these key individuals early in the strategic sales process.

The second step will be to demonstrate compelling business value to the organisation, and legitimate personal value to the individual influencer, if there is to be any chance of harnessing their personal support. To achieve that position, the Business Consultant and the Relationship Manager's roles will again need to combine their respective strategic insight, to create a compelling value proposition which is focused on each potential supporter's business and personal agenda.

Let's take another look at the status of the relationships for each of the three customers you have selected:

APPLY THE PLAYBOOK – 10

Key Individuals – My Relationships Status (2)

How many **active** individual relationships do you have with each of your selected customers currently?

How many **active** individual relationships do you have with each of the important business and service units currently?

At what level in the organisational hierarchy is each individual? How many are there now at the board level? How many are there now at the management level? How many are there now at the operational level?

$\rightarrow$

Have you identified the strategic decision-makers?

Have you decided how you will gain access to each of the decision-makers?

Have you identified "credible influencers" who can support you in gaining access to the decision-makers?

What business and personal value can you provide for them that will harness their support?

How will you make the idea of a value-based partnership attractive to these key individuals?

Have you asked your key contacts recently, "Who else in the organisation should I talk to?"

A Tricky Question

I want to make one final and important point about the level of influence we as salespeople must also bring to the sales process.

I often ask account managers whether or not they themselves should be in the customer's DMU as a key influencer. The question is normally greeted by a blank stare, as everybody believes it's a trick question!

However, there are always a few who get the message I'm trying to convey: that we have to see our role as a key influencer in the customer's decision-making process or we are not really doing our job as a Sales Strategist.

If that is a role we must perform to be consistently successful, then what do we need to demonstrate in order to take that position of influence?

Let's go back to the three characteristics of influence we introduced earlier in this chapter and apply them to ourselves.

Expertise

Can you demonstrate a credible level of business acumen when discussing the customer's business, its marketplace and its key business objectives? Can you display a similar level of expert knowledge of your marketplace and your products and services?

Track Record

Can you prove your organisation's ability to deliver effective business solutions to the customer by referencing past successes dealing with similar issues with other customers?

Personal Relationships

Can you show that you can translate expert business knowledge and insight and apply that insight to the business and personal agendas of key individuals?

The more of these personal attributes you can demonstrate to those individuals in the DMU, the more likely you are to gain influence and decisive leverage in the customer's decision-making process.

CHAPTER SEVEN

The Competitor Analyst

> "If an executive does not employ inside informants and consultants to discover his competitor's strengths and weaknesses, he cannot create successful plans".
> —Donald Krause, *The Art of War for Executives*

The Business Consultant and the Relationship Manager have done a great job up to this point of providing the Sales Strategist with two important perspectives:

1. How our targeted customers define strategic success for their organisations
2. The identities of those individuals that either decide or influence the strategic decision-making process

In researching the customer's strategic business environment and identifying and meeting with the key individuals, the names and identities of competitors would have begun to emerge.

It is at this point that the role of the Competitor Analyst will start to make an initial but important contribution to the

Sales Strategist's insight into the overall sales environment. The competitors' names will have been identified and some initial questions asked to determine the competitive status of each individual competitor.

A sales manager once summed up his attitude toward his competitors by saying that when he was competing for a customer's or prospect's business he saw his own strategic position as either "outside looking in" or "inside looking out". The way he saw the competitive landscape was that he was in a sales position which either needed to be defended, "inside looking out", or in a position from which he needed to attack, "outside looking in".

His rationale for seeing things this way was that it ensured that he never overlooked the fact that he was operating in a competitive environment that was essentially predatory in nature.

Competitors – Why Bother?

Some salespeople feel that giving this level of attention to their competitors is somehow displaying a sign of weakness or a lack of confidence in their organisation's products and services.

On the contrary – it is a vitally important part of how the Sales Strategist needs to operate. How can you gain a competitive advantage if you have little or no competitive insight? How can you differentiate your solutions from your competitors' solutions if you have no actual knowledge of their offerings?

Sun Tzu said in *The Art of War,* "Know the enemy and know yourself; in a hundred battles you will never be in peril".

Michael Corleone in *The Godfather* said, "There are many things my father taught me here in this room. He taught me: keep your friends close, but your enemies closer".

So what the Sales Manager, Sun Tzu and Michael

Corleone were all saying was that you really need to act like a well-informed general.

> "Like the general, you must recognise that your business rivals...are intelligent and purposeful people".
> —Dixit and Nalebuff, *Thinking Strategically*

The role of the Competitor Analyst is therefore to analyse and assess each competitor strategically:

- Who are our rivals?
- Are they "like-for-like" or niche competitors?
- What are their major strengths?
- What are their major weaknesses?
- What action do we need to take to differentiate ourselves by exploiting our competitors' major weaknesses?
- What action do we need to take to insulate ourselves against their major strengths?

These insights enable the Competitor Analyst to outthink the competition and formulate strategies that will outmanoeuvre them.

In the movie *Patton*, we see a very good example of how timely and accurate intelligence enables successful strategies. With his formidable aggression and unrelenting discipline, General George S. Patton managed to put US forces back on the offensive after a series of defeats, winning the second world war's first major American victory against Rommel's Afrika Corp in the Battle of El Guettar in March 1943.

Prior to this pivotal battle, there is a scene in which Patton is awakened by his aides and told that US intelligence has discovered that the legendary German general, Rommel, is on the move and is planning to attack the US forces at El Guettar. As the camera pans back from Patton's bed, it settles for a brief moment on his bedside table and the book he has been reading. Its title is *The Tank in Attack*, by Erwin Rommel.

Later, as Patton surveys the carnage of the battle in which he and his army were victorious, he utters the words, "Rommel...you magnificent bastard, *I read your book!*

To outthink and outmanoeuvre Rommel, Patton relied heavily on accurate intelligence from two perspectives. The first perspective was gained from his intelligence experts – that Rommel was on the move and also where he would confront the US forces. The second perspective was gained from Rommel's book, where Patton learned the likely tactics that his rival would use in the battle itself.

Accurate Information leads to Effective Strategies

Effective strategies are a function of how much accurate information we have about the competitive environment. We don't want to launch a sales strategy based on incomplete or inaccurate information that may fail as a consequence.

Here is an illustration of where accurate information about competitors provided one account manager with a decisive edge.

I was working with a group of account managers from a major telecom client. One of the major sales issues we were addressing was the need to differentiate your solutions from your competitor's solutions.

We had discussed a number of points, among which was the need to be fully acquainted with the customer's requirements, but also with the corresponding competitive solutions that were being offered. The key point that was being made was that differentiation is situational and not generic. Uniqueness, we had agreed, should be a function of what is needed to satisfy a specific customer's requirements, on understanding the actual scope of each competitor's capabilities – unique situation by unique situation.

One of the account managers then proceeded to present his solution which highlighted a unique feature. In the ensuing feedback session, his colleagues started to harangue him about the validity of this unique feature. They told him that there were other suppliers that could offer this particular functionality, so he should not be highlighting it as unique.

His response was to agree with them – in part. He said that they were correct about those competitors that could offer that same functionality. However, he also said that he knew, on this particular occasion, that he was not competing with these particular rivals. The companies he was competing with could not offer that functionality, and so he felt quite within his rights to promote that capability as unique.

He was absolutely correct. There is a real competitive advantage available to those who utilise the Competitor Analyst's skills effectively.

In the previous chapter we looked at how the Business Consultant role and the Relationship Manager role worked together to produce the insight that helped us focus on the most strategic individuals across the customer's organisation. Now we will see how both the Business Consultant and the Relationship Manager need to work with the Competitor Analyst – to gather the competitive intelligence vital to promoting a strategic, value-based proposition that differentiates us from other suppliers.

The first objective for the Competitor Analyst will be to identify each active competitor engaged in winning or trying to win business from each targeted customer. It's important to get a clear perspective on each competitor's strategic position as quickly as possible.

APPLY THE PLAYBOOK – 11

The Competitive Landscape (1)

Review the competitive landscape for each of the three customers you have selected.

→

Who are your **active** competitors?

What general marketplace information do we have about these competitors? Products and services? Market coverage and status? Years in business? Strength of their brands?

For each target customer, are they inside looking out or are they outside looking in?

In which business and service units are they active?

Do they have an installed base of products and services?

What information have you gathered about the current level of customer satisfaction with their performance? What do the key individuals tell you?

At this initial assessment stage, what do you see as the strengths and weaknesses of your competitors?

The answers to these "first pass" questions will show us how much we really know about the competitive landscape in our high-potential accounts.

If our preferred sales approach is transactional, then some of the questions would be difficult to answer confidently without further research. If our preferred sales approach is strategic, then most of the questions should be fairly easy to answer.

Another important question we need to answer is illustrated by Patton's purpose in reading Rommel's book. He wanted to know what Rommel's likely preferred strategy would be so he could be ready to respond with a counter strategy of his own – that he already knew would create a winning position for him and his troops.

History Repeating Itself

A similar question the Competitor Analyst will ask is, "How does my competitor's sales approach with this customer compare to their sales approach elsewhere?"

Are they transactional and not strategic? Do they always sell on price? Are their customer relationships normally at the lower levels of the organisation?

If we can identify our competitors' preferred sales strategy, it becomes far easier to anticipate their tactics and, like Patton, set our competitive strategy in place to neutralise them and make decisive progress ourselves.

"Smart executives employ only the most capable people in their intelligence networks. It is through these people that they achieve success. Intelligence is the essence and foundation of all competitive actions".
— Donald G. Krause, *The Art of War for Executives*

A key area of intelligence-gathering, where the Relationship Manager and the Competitor Analyst can work together, is in understanding where competitors have established their current relationships. A competitor's level of competitive advantage can be most accurately assessed once you have a clear picture of the level and quality of their coverage strategy.

Some transactional competitors reveal themselves very quickly, by targeting only one element of the customer's business. For example, technology companies may focus almost entirely on the IT department, training organisations will focus mainly on human resources and PR and advertising consultants might well focus on the marketing department.

This kind of narrow focus and coverage will mean that these competitors are likely to have a very limited view of their customer's strategic goals and objectives. This narrow perspective will make it extremely difficult for them to demonstrate any significant strategic value or develop the all-important longer-term value-based partnerships.

They will also be overlooking and probably ignoring some very important individuals, some of whom will play an active and pivotal role in the strategic decision-making process.

With the Business Consultant's and the Relationship Manager's contribution already in place, the Competitor Analyst should be able to quite easily exploit any competitor with restricted coverage and inadequate strategic insight.

It is worth noting at this point that one of the most frequent challenges facing salespeople who want to change their sales approach from being far less transactional to becoming far more strategic is how to expand their current limited coverage. Salespeople in this position frequently become concerned about damaging their current relationships which are probably at too low a level or are restricted to one or two service units. Their concern is centred on how their current supporters will react when they feel that they are no longer at the centre of the salesperson's attention.

Whilst coverage expansion is frequently necessary, some care needs to be taken to ensure that this kind of situation is dealt with thoughtfully to avoid turning a motivated supporter into a demotivated adversary. The key principle here is keeping the focus on the expansion of coverage we need but at the same time reconnecting that change of direction to the personal agendas of our existing supporters.

What additional value will they derive from our wider coverage?

The Secret Assassins

Up to this point we have focused on our "real" competitors. A "real" competitor is one actively selling similar products and services to the same customers as we are.

However, there are two other competitors which we will describe as "virtual" competitors. These two competitors have probably cost us more unproductive time and wasted energy than any of our real competitors. We have probably "lost" more business to these two competitors than to all of our "real" competitors combined.

I call them the "secret assassins", and a transactional account manager will be easily beguiled and outwitted by them. The Sales Strategist, on the other hand, will be well aware of their existence and the negative impact they can have on the unsuspecting account manager's valuable time and resources.

We will identify these two competitors, the secret assassins, as "AUC" and "BAU".

AUC is the **Alternate Use of Capital** and represents the other internal customer projects and programmes competing with us for the customer's cash investment and organisational resources.

There will be always other internal projects or plans that are seen by the customer as more mission-critical. In contrast, there will be some market challenges that will not be perceived as important enough to justify any corporate action. In these circumstances it would be clearly irresponsible to waste valuable time and resources pursuing these issues as legitimate sales opportunities when the customer's strategic focus is elsewhere.

BAU is **Business As Usual** and represents the customer's decision to do nothing in the face of the external business challenges that directly impact the organization.

In this situation, a "no-decision" represents a real lack of insight on the part of the salesperson. Pursuing these unqualified "phantom" opportunities is another real waste of time and energy.

In Chapter Five, we saw that one of the key activities of the Business Consultant was to qualify the mission-critical nature of these kinds of challenges to the organisation's strategic success before embarking on a sales campaign to nowhere!

APPLY THE PLAYBOOK – 12

The Competitive Landscape (2)

Review once more your competitive status with each of your selected customers.

How many of your competitors have preferred and predictable sales strategies?

Are any of your competitors focusing their coverage on only one or two service units?

At what organisational level are their individual relationships?

How much competitive advantage do these relationships provide for each of them?

How will you outthink and outmanoeuvre them?

Have you discovered any "virtual" competitors that could challenge you on any of the current or emerging sales opportunities you've identified?

What are the key strengths of your active competitors?

How will you insulate yourself against them?

What are their key weaknesses?

How will you exploit those weaknesses and create competitive advantage?

SWOT It!

A very useful and popular tool which enables us to organise our strategic information into a manageable structure for both analysis and decision-making purposes is the SWOT analysis.

> "What makes SWOT particularly powerful is that, with a little thought, it can help you uncover opportunities that you are well-placed to exploit. And by understanding the weaknesses of your business, you can manage and eliminate threats that would otherwise catch you unawares".
> —MindTools

For a Sales Strategist, a SWOT analysis is fairly simple to use. For a transactional salesperson, it may well be tough to use it to develop any truly meaningful insight. Let's apply it to our three selected customers.

APPLY THE PLAYBOOK – 13

The SWOT Analysis

Review all of the strategic intelligence you have gathered so far for your three selected customers.

Focus on the customer's business, the key relationships and the competitive landscape.

Where do your strengths lie for each high-potential customer?

Where are your weaknesses?

→

How can you leverage your strengths and develop competitive advantage?

How can you insulate yourself against any weaknesses
being exploited by your competitors?

Whatever your sales approach, a truly objective application of a SWOT analysis will challenge your level of strategic awareness for each customer. At the same time, it will reveal some of the priority actions that you need to take to strengthen your overall strategic position with each key customer.

However, it is important to keep any SWOT analysis in perspective, so make sure that you:

- Keep the analysis short and simple.
- Try to avoid creating too much complexity.
- Use the analysis as a guide and not a prescription when you are deciding on any subsequent actions you need to take.

Another word of caution at this point is that in the process of gathering competitive intelligence, the Competitor Analyst will, from time to time, confront the Sales Strategist with a challenging situation.

Let's say you become aware that because a competitor has such a strong and embedded position with a particular customer, you cannot succeed now or in the foreseeable future, no matter how resourceful and creative you are.

This situation should not be viewed as a failure but more of a "blinding flash of reality". You will need to decide whether to continue to compete in a "mission near-impossible" situation or "qualify out" of this particular sales campaign.

Can you redirect your sales energy and resources more productively elsewhere? It's your judgement, it's your call.

The decisions we make here are all related to the

important principle of opportunity cost which we covered in Chapter Five.

If you are operating as a Sales Strategist, you will be able to use the intelligence gathered by the Business Consultant, the Relationship Manager and the Competitor Analyst to make informed decisions about where you can generate the best return on investment from the application of your sales resources.

If you are operating at a transactional level, then it's anybody's guess!

"A leader who knows when to fight and when to retreat will win".
—Donald Krause, *The Art of War for Executives*

CHAPTER EIGHT

The Solution Provider

"Your prospects have one basic question: What makes
you so different that I should do business with you? Your
prospects are making the classic statement: Give me one
good reason why."
—Harry Beckwith, *Selling the Invisible*

With the contribution of three of the four key roles, the
Sales Strategist is now in a very advantageous position from
which to build robust, value-based partnerships with customers, and to dominate the competitive environment.

Through disciplined research, the Business Consultant
has been able to put a powerful spotlight on the customer's
business situation – in particular, its business strategy for
the achievement of its short-, medium- and longer-term
success. That research will also have highlighted many of the
opportunities, challenges and problems that will confront
the customer in their continuing pursuit of commercial
success.

At the same time, the Relationship Manager has
identified those customer executives and managers
commonly referred to as the "key players". These are the

individuals who play a pivotal role in deciding on the kinds of business initiatives and interventions that need to be implemented to grasp the opportunities, overcome the challenges and solve the problems.

The interventions and initiatives selected by the "key players" for implementation will normally focus on those business issues that will make the biggest impact, negatively or positively, on the organisation's quest for success. In a similar fashion, by gathering and assessing accurate intelligence, the Competitor Analyst has been able to assess the level of advantage attained by each potential competitor.

How well do the various competitors understand the customer's strategic position? What degree of insight do they actually possess? What quality of relationship does each one have with the key individuals? How much leverage do they have as a result?

These three roles have provided the Sales Strategist with a potentially powerful platform of insight and subsequent advantage from which real progress can be made.

However, now the Sales Strategist needs to call on the assistance of the fourth role – the Solution Provider – if our overall competitive strategy is to be fully energised and wholly effective.

Can We Really Compete?

Do we possess the appropriate answers, capabilities or resources that will make it possible for the customer to capitalise on the opportunities, overcome the challenges and solve the problems that will lead them to strategic success?

At this is the point in the sales process, it is crucial that a strategic perspective is maintained, and great care needs to be exercised not to lower our sales horizon to that of the transactional salesperson.

The inherent danger is that we view our overall capabilities in such a way as to undermine our eventual ability to contribute to our customers that most precious of all sales commodities: *unique business value.*

The transactional salesperson frequently views business value as not much more than a commodity product, a discounted price and a delivery date. All too frequently their attempts to demonstrate business value to well-informed customers turn out to be little more than a product and price tour through their organisation's brochure.

In contrast, the Sales Strategist has a much more expansive view of their organisation's capabilities. That expansive perspective carries with it a major opportunity to create decisive competitive advantage.

So what is this expanded view of our organisations' capabilities? What kind of thinking process do you need to adopt if you are going to create compelling business value for your customers?

Here's my definition of a business solution:

"A business solution is an idea, a product or a service which enables an organisation to capitalise on an opportunity, overcome a challenge or resolve a problem successfully'".

In simple terms, the Solution Provider's role is to construct and craft business solutions that will address the customer's key strategic issues identified by the Business Consultant. However, in order to achieve this high level of sustainable and strategic impact, the Solution Provider will have to focus on far more than just the organisation's core products and services.

They will have to reach out across their whole organisation and harness any and all of its capabilities that contribute the relevant business value to the customer – independent of the price tag.

Don't Be a Dinosaur

Logically, we should start by assessing our core products and services and first analyse their potential customer value.

Then we should reach out across our organisation and add to that initial assessment by taking a more strategic view of our company's capabilities.

Even at this most basic of sales perspectives, the Solution Provider takes a fundamentally different view to that of the transactional salesperson. The transactional salesperson usually has a very thorough knowledge of the technical specifications and the key features of their products and services. They may even have strong, historical relationships with their customers as a result of their technical prowess.

However, the impact this kind of transactional salesperson has on their customers will become progressively weaker. We have already seen that customers are now actively seeking out "value-based partnerships" with suppliers. Whilst technical capability is clearly important, the specific, measurable business value that is delivered to the customer is now, by far, the highest priority.

The transactional salesperson will progressively become the "dinosaur" of professional sales, because they will continue to rely far too heavily on their technical expertise and the mistaken belief that their technical knowledge is still the most important component of their sales "pitch". In contrast, the Solution Provider will turn this product knowledge and technical expertise "on its head".

They understand the need to define and position all their products and services in a way that always highlights their potential business value. Every product feature has been assessed and its clear potential to deliver real business value designed into every tailored sales presentation – business value first, product feature second!

There are many examples of organisations that have leveraged a clear product and price advantage and have gained considerable market share as a result. In the European and the US supermarket sectors, Aldi offers a wide range of products increasingly seen by many consumers to be comparable to established brands and offered at much lower "budget" prices. This lower-cost retail strategy has enabled Aldi to grow exponentially over recent years.

Likewise, Easyjet and Ryanair are European airlines who, like Frontier and Southwest in the US market, have revolutionised air travel with their "no frills, low cost" flights.

The message is clear: if you have clearly competitive product and price features, you must leverage those benefits and create as much competitive advantage and customer value as possible.

Here's how one financial services business consultant changed his mindset, took a different approach and got a great result.

I was working with a major British bank that wanted to bring an upgraded level of professional selling to its national team of business services consultants. We had already covered, in previous workshops, most of the core sales skills and activities that the team needed for the upgrade, and now we had regrouped to review the personal progress that each consultant had made in implementing some of the new sales approaches.

There were, as always in these kinds of sessions, some great stories and anecdotes of commercial success and personal growth. However, one story in particular made a real impression on me and the whole group.

The consultant told us of how he had been given the responsibility of introducing two new bank products to potential business prospects in his territory. He emphasized that these prospects were genuine new business targets and not current clients of the bank.

He went on to say that his first objective was to get an appointment with each prospect for a meeting in which he could spend quality time doing some face-to-face selling.

His normal approach, he said, would have been very "product-focused" when making that initial telephone call. He would make the call, equipped with all of the product's features, and then try to convince the prospect that this product was something about which they should really learn more. Then, at an opportune moment, he would try to make the appointment.

On this occasion, he tried a very different method, inspired by the value-based approach we had covered in our workshops. A major part of his pre-call planning was to take each product in turn, identifying their key features and asking a very simple question:

"What business problems or challenges would I be facing that would make this product and its features the most likely solution?"

Having identified the typical business challenges and problems, he then crafted some related consultative questions that he would ask his prospect to lead off his telephone call. His simple objective was to discover if his prospect was, in fact, experiencing those issues for which he already knew his product was a potential solution.

Using this approach, he simply asked for 60 minutes of his prospect's time, to discuss in more detail how he could help address those business issues.

He concluded his story by telling us his "strike rate" – how many of his initial telephone calls he had converted into face-to-face meetings – was 100 percent!

Leading with the business value of your products and services makes such a huge difference.

APPLY THE PLAYBOOK – 14

Building the Solution – Products and Services

Think about your three high-potential customers and their needs.

Analyse the features and pricing of your most appropriate products and services.

What are the typical business challenges and problems that each product or service can resolve?

Reassess your competitors' offerings and pricing.

Identify where you believe you have a product or price advantage that is not only *relevant* to meeting the customer's needs but also provides you with competitive advantage.

How will you highlight the business value in your customer pitches?

However, for most organisations, promoting unique products or heavily discounted pricing will be neither a viable nor a desirable option in the search for sustainable competitive advantage.

"We will never try to develop a strategy based on pricing; there is nothing unique about pricing".
—Josh Weston, former CEO of ADP, global provider of human capital management

---

So if your product and price advantage is neither a decisive nor a viable option, then the Solution Provider will need to look elsewhere for that additional customer value and competitive advantage.

Customer-Facing Processes and Systems

One place to look is at the different methods we use to engage with customers during and after the sales process. Every organisation has processes and systems designed to make it easier and more convenient to do business with customers.

Placing and processing orders, installation expertise, 24/7 support, technical training and product maintenance are well-known methods whereby organisations add considerable value to their core services and products.

The Internet is a great example of how a "process" has transformed the world of buying and selling. It has brought into play a completely different and compelling method of continuous interaction with customers. Vast numbers of organisations now use the Internet to promote, offer, sell and deliver their products and services to customers anytime, anywhere in the world.

E-commerce has provided an exciting and profitable way for organisations to do business with their customers. Equally, customers have found these Web-based processes to be hugely convenient and a significant time-saver.

> "Make your product easier to buy than your competition, or you will find your customers buying from them, not you".
> —Mark Cuban, US entrepreneur

Organisations like Amazon, eBay, Facebook and LinkedIn have all built market-leading positions by leveraging powerful technology-driven processes to deliver consistent levels of service and ongoing support for their customers. UK supermarket Tesco has also enhanced its online ordering system with home deliveries – yet another process that adds an additional layer of customer value in the form of more convenience and greater time-saving.

APPLY THE PLAYBOOK – 15

Building the Solution – Processes

Review your high-potential customers and their strategic needs.

Analyse the features of your organisational processes or systems.

Which ones make it easier for your customers to do business with you?

How might they enhance the measurable business value your customer will receive?

How can you highlight the value of these processes and systems in your solutions?

How might they help you to differentiate yourself from your competitors?

The Solution Provider knows that when we take our core products and our customer-facing business processes and embed them together into our solutions, we create additional attractive business value for our customers. As a bonus, at the same time we can also develop some serious competitive advantage for ourselves.

Suppose we could add even more business value into this initial mix of products and processes. How much more compelling would our solutions become? What increased levels of competitive differentiation could we develop?

The Solution Provider knows that there is a considerable amount of additional business value and competitive advantage that can be uncovered in two other areas of organisational life: internal and external to the organisation.

Our People Are Power

"It never ceases to amaze me how many businesses give away their expertise for free. What's more, they give it away in such a manner that their clients don't even value it".
— David Finkel, *Seven Proven Principles to Grow Your Business and Get Your Life Back*

The internal focuses on *our people,* whose skills, talents and experience can add significant business value to our solutions and will augment the value we have already identified in our core products and business processes.

Many organisations present their complete offering in the form of their people. Professional service organisations like management consultancies, architects, auditors, engineers, doctors and lawyers can frequently embody, in their employees, almost the totality of the business value of their organisations.

We need to pay particular attention to the technical skills, the proven expertise and the track record of all the talented individuals throughout our organisations – they can frequently provide us with additional customer value and even more competitive advantage.

APPLY THE PLAYBOOK – 16

Building the Solution – People

Review your high-potential customers and their strategic needs.

Identify those individuals in your organisation that have skills, experience and expertise relevant to your customers' needs.

Which individuals will provide your customers with high-class, specialist value?

What can you do to promote their specialised skills and talents to your customers?

How will you embed their expertise into your business solutions?

How can you leverage their expertise and create differentiation from your competitors?

Our Partner Network

The Solution Provider is fully aware that being strategic will mean not just looking inside your own organisation, but also outside, in the continuous search for incremental business value and competitive advantage. The external area that can contribute additional business value and increased competitive advantage is through your *partner network.*

"Partnerships between people, between companies, with customers and with suppliers create greater value for all concerned".
—Stanley C. Gault, CEO and Chairman, Goodyear Tire and Rubber Company, 1991–1996

Computer companies promote Intel, EBay promotes PayPal, high street stores offer credit card payments, airlines promote car hire companies and washing machine companies promote detergents – all of these represent well-known "partnerships" and can provide real incremental value for the primary supplier's customers.

One of my clients uses a third-party logistics company to deliver their products to major construction sites throughout the UK. Many of the construction companies demand compliance with some very challenging health and safety protocols on their sites. Some also insist on the observation of tough environmental codes.

Unlike some of their competitors, my client had always seen these issues as a vitally important "quality of service" criterion when selecting their partners. Having logistics partners that had trained and accredited their staff in all of the legislative requirements of health and safety was a significant advantage.

The added benefit of their environmental qualifications added even more impact, creating additional business value for their customers and competitive advantage for themselves. Their area sales managers naturally paid a lot of attention to promoting the benefits of their partners wherever it was relevant – in their tailored business solutions, their marketing materials, their customer meetings and their business proposals.

APPLY THE PLAYBOOK – 17

Building the Solution – Partners

Review your high-potential customers and their strategic needs.

Identify those business partners with relevant products, processes and people.

How can they provide your customers with incremental and specialist value?

What can you do to promote their specialised capabilities to your customers?

How can you integrate their unique value into your business solutions?

How can you leverage their credentials and expertise and differentiate yourself from your competitors?

So the role of the Solution Provider is to promote an expanded, more strategic view of those capabilities that our organisation can embed into their business solutions – utilising every bit of relevant and appropriate business value that can be identified via *our products, our processes, our people and our partners.*

One More Thing...

An important factor to bear in mind when promoting or pitching our solutions is the mindset of the decision-maker or key influencer to whom we are presenting our business solution. No matter how great a job we've done up until now, a prospect or a lapsed customer will always have some sense of potential risk in their minds.

"Am I making the right choice?" "Can I trust this organisation to perform in line with what they've told me?"

Anecdotes, testimonials and case studies significantly reduce this fear of the unknown in any customer's mind. They help to create the credibility and confidence needed for our prospect to say "Yes" to switching their business to us.

"Tell me a fact and I'll learn. Tell me the truth and I'll believe. Tell me a story and it will live in my heart forever".
—Indian proverb

Here are some guidelines to help make sure anecdotes and case studies work for us:

- Ensure the business issue at the heart of our message is identical or very similar to the one we are addressing with our customer or prospect. Relevance is vital.
- Identify the customer, the subject of the story, wherever possible. Our story has to be real. If naming the customer is not possible, then we will need to select a similar or identical market sector.
- Highlight the measurable payoff the customer enjoyed by switching their business to us. There has to be some measurable business value – the all-important "what's in it for me" factor.

APPLY THE PLAYBOOK – 18

Case Studies and Anecdotes

Review your high-potential customers and their strategic needs.

Where have you successfully delivered solutions in the past that met identical or similar needs?

Will those customers agree to be a referral or provide you with a testimonial?

Does your organisation have up-to-date and relevant case studies that you can use?

Who are the individuals in your customers' organisations who might be influenced by case studies and anecdotes?

How will you present the message to them?

In this chapter, we have explored the role of the Solution Provider – a role that challenges us to develop a far broader perspective of our organisation's capabilities than just focusing on our core products and services.

We have seen that a broader perspective is incredibly important if we are genuinely intent on building more resilient, more value-based partnerships with our high-potential customers and creating that all-important competitive advantage for ourselves.

"The need to sell more than the product requires an enormous change in emphasis in most companies...the traditional sales force that sold just the product is going to be at a distinct disadvantage".
—John Rock, *Key Account Management*

CHAPTER NINE

Moving Forward

"The challenge for selling companies in sustaining partnerships is to keep raising the bar of account management achievement in order to realize business growth in the future".
—McDonald, Rogers and Woodburn, *Key Customers – How to Manage Them Profitably*

The four roles of the Sales Strategist that have formed the basis of most of this book provide you with a formidable sales infrastructure. The strategic perspective that this position provides will enable you to make more effective decisions about managing your personal sales environment.

The insight you gain will provide you with the direction and focus you need to make every sales interaction with your customers far more productive and certainly far more value-based. You will be able to shape and build value-based partnerships that will fuel your business development, expand your pipeline and, most important of all, grow your business profitably.

Throughout this book I have invited you, from time to time, to "Apply the Playbook". It's vital that we don't just "know right things", but also "do right things".

We will need to keep track of the changes across our strategic sales environment by using a consistent process. In this way we can adjust our sales strategies when necessary and ensure that we stay on course. Only then do we really learn; only then will good things happen for us more and more frequently.

To make your ongoing reviews easier to manage, I have put all the "Apply the Playbook" activities in one place.

Each of the activities and the corresponding questions will, I believe, improve the quality of your decisions about the most effective way forward in your particular sales environment.

Become more strategic – see more, understand more, win more!

APPLY THE PLAYBOOK – 1

Availability of Potential Future Revenue

Where is growth to be found?

Taking each customer in turn, ask:

Has the customer discussed and clarified their strategic business goals and key objectives with you?

Has the customer confirmed that business growth is one of their key objectives?

Are the current trends in the customer's key market sector(s) positive?

Is the customer a market leader whose reputation other organisations respect?

Is the customer's overall financial status in a healthy state?

(Has the customer put specific marketing programmes in place to support its strategic business plans and key objectives?)

Has the customer identified any major challenges that stand in the way of achieving their goal and objectives?

Can you identify early opportunities for your business solutions?

Have you validated the accuracy of your responses above with at least three key individuals across the customer's organisation?

To review the background information for this exercise, go to Chapter Four.

APPLY THE PLAYBOOK – 2

Accessibility of Potential Future Revenue

Can you access the growth potential?

Taking each customer in turn, ask:

Do you have an installed base of products and services?

Do you have access to and credible relationships with the customer's strategic decision-makers and influencers?

Does your range of business solutions align with the customer's future business plans and key objectives?

Do you have validated evidence that the customer's current level of satisfaction with your organisation is positive?

Do recent SWOT analyses on each of your key competitors confirm that you have sufficient competitive advantage?

Do you have sufficient resources to create and develop additional new business over the medium and longer term?

Have you validated the accuracy of your responses above with key personnel in your own organisation?

To review the background information for this exercise, go to Chapter Four.

APPLY THE PLAYBOOK – 3

Selecting My High-Potential Customers

Review the results of Apply the Playbook 1 and 2.

Select six of your customers/prospects that you believe are now worthy of some business development activity.

Now re-examine each of the assessments and decide on four or five actions for each customer, to either retrieve missing information or to confirm *with evidence* the positive responses.

Set a deadline of no more than 30 days to complete all the actions.

Once all the actions are completed, review the six customers/prospects again.

Decide which *three* customers/prospects you believe reveal the most positive indications of new business potential.

Decide which *three* customers reflect positive indicators of a potential value-based partnership.

To review the background information for this exercise, go to Chapter Four.

APPLY THE PLAYBOOK – 4

My Customers' Strategic Goals

Focus only on those customers you have selected in Apply the Playbook 3.

Do you know the longer-term goal of each high-potential customer you have selected?

Have you confirmed with key individuals in each organisation that their goal plays an integral and active part in their business strategy?

If you are clear about your customer's goal, what initial opportunity can you see to contribute strategic value?

If not, which information sources will you use to gain a clearer understanding of each customer's strategic goal?

What relevant case studies or testimonials can demonstrate your organisation's track record in enabling other customers to achieve these kinds of goals?

To review the background information for this exercise, go to Chapter Five.

APPLY THE PLAYBOOK – 5

My Customers' Key Objectives

Review the goals of your selected high-potential customers

Using the SMART process, describe each customer's shorter-term objectives that are connected to the achievement of their longer-term goals.

From the insight you have now gained, which business and service units have a higher level of strategic importance in accomplishing each customer's goal?

Using SMART, describe the objectives of those strategically important business and service units.

Which units could provide current and future sales opportunities for you?

What testimonials do you have that prove your organisation provides business solutions that can help to achieve these kinds of objectives?

To review the background information for this exercise, go to Chapter Five.

APPLY THE PLAYBOOK – 6

External Factors and Challenges

Review your three selected customers.

Using the PESTLE approach, identify those external market factors *currently* impacting your three selected customers.

Identify any additional external factors where the impact on the customer will be over *the medium/longer term.*

Which external factors will provide the most significant challenges?

Which business and service units will be affected the most?

Where can you identify current or emerging opportunities for your products and services?

What testimonials do you have that demonstrate your organisation's track record in dealing with these kinds of challenges?

To review the background information for this exercise, go to Chapter Five.

APPLY THE PLAYBOOK – 7

Internal Factors and Challenges

Review your three selected customers.

Using the SPIESO approach, identify any internal factors currently impacting your three selected customers.

Which internal pressures will provide the most significant challenges?

Which business and service units will be affected the most?

What current or emerging opportunities can you identify for your products and services?

What testimonials do you have that demonstrate your organisation's track record in providing business solutions that address these kinds of challenges?

To review the background information for this exercise, go to Chapter Five.

APPLY THE PLAYBOOK – 8

Interim Strategic Review

Review your position (the strategic status) with each of your three selected customers.

Is your initial assessment of the long-term value of each customer still valid?

How many current and potential sales opportunities have you identified?

Which business and service units are now your priority targets?

What is their overall estimated value?

Are you satisfied with your potential Return on Investment?

For each customer, which business and service units are your priority targets?

What actions do you need to take to retrieve missing or incomplete information?

Who will you meet with in order to validate and prioritise the intelligence you have gathered so far?

To review the background information for this exercise, go to Chapters One to Five.

APPLY THE PLAYBOOK – 9

Key Individuals – My Relationships Status (1)

Review your individual relationship status with each of the three customers you have selected.

Based on the McGraw-Hill research, how many individuals do you believe are likely to be in the Decision Making Unit (DMU) for each of your three selected customers?

How many **active** individual relationships do you have with each of your selected customers?

How many **active** individual relationships do you have with each of the important business and service units?

How many are at the board level? How many are at management level? How many are at the supervisory or operational level?

With which executives and senior managers do you need to arrange meetings?

Is the quality of your strategic research relevant and sufficient enough to provide a compelling reason for those executives or senior managers to spend time with you?

***To review the background information for this exercise,
go to Chapter Six.***

APPLY THE PLAYBOOK – 10

Key Individuals – My Relationships Status (2)

How many **active** individual relationships do you have with each of your selected customers currently?

How many **active** individual relationships do you have with each of the important business and service units currently?

At what level in the organisational hierarchy is each individual? How many are there now at the board level? How many are there now at the management level? How many are there now at the operational level?

Have you identified the strategic decision-makers?

Have you decided how you will gain access to each of the decision-makers?

Have you identified "credible influencers" who can support you in gaining access to the decision-makers?

What business and personal value can you provide for them that will harness their support?

How will you make the idea of a value-based partnership attractive to these key individuals?

Have you asked your key contacts recently, "Who else in the organisation should I talk to?"

To review the background information for this exercise, go to Chapter Six.

APPLY THE PLAYBOOK – 11

The Competitive Landscape (1)

Review the competitive landscape for each of the three customers you have selected.

Who are your **active** competitors?

What general marketplace information do we have about these competitors? Products and services? Market coverage and status? Years in business? Strength of their brands?

For each target customer, are they inside looking out or are they outside looking in?

In which business and service units are they active?

Do they have an installed base of products and services?

What information have you gathered about the current level of customer satisfaction with their performance? What do the key individuals tell you?

At this initial assessment stage, what do you see as the strengths and weaknesses of your competitors?

To review the background information for this exercise, go to Chapter Seven.

APPLY THE PLAYBOOK – 12

The Competitive Landscape (2)

Review once more your competitive status with each of your selected customers.

How many of your competitors have preferred and predictable sales strategies?

Are any of your competitors focusing their coverage on only one or two service units?

At what organisational level are their individual relationships?

How much competitive advantage do these relationships provide for each of them?

How will you outthink and outmanoeuvre them?

Have you discovered any "virtual" competitors that could challenge you on any of the current or emerging sales opportunities you've identified?

What are the key strengths of your active competitors?

How will you insulate yourself against them?

What are their key weaknesses?

How will you exploit those weaknesses and create competitive advantage?

To review the background information for this exercise,
go to Chapter Seven.

APPLY THE PLAYBOOK – 13

The SWOT Analysis

Review all of the strategic intelligence you have gathered so far for your three selected customers.

Focus on the customer's business, the key relationships and the competitive landscape.

Where do your strengths lie for each high-potential customer?

Where are your weaknesses?

How can you leverage your strengths and develop competitive advantage?

How can you insulate yourself against any weaknesses being exploited by your competitors?

To review the background information for this exercise, go to Chapter Seven.

APPLY THE PLAYBOOK – 14

Building the Solution – Products and Services

Think about your three high-potential customers and their needs.

Analyse the features and pricing of your most relevant products and services.

What are the typical business challenges and problems that each product or service can resolve?

Reassess your competitors' offerings and pricing.

Identify where you believe you have a product or price advantage that is not only *relevant* to meeting the customer's needs but also provides you with competitive advantage.

How will you highlight the business value in your customer pitches?

To review the background information for this exercise, go to Chapter Eight.

APPLY THE PLAYBOOK – 15

Building the Solution – Processes

Review your high-potential customers and their strategic needs.

Analyse the features of your organisational processes or systems.

Which ones make it easier for your customers to do business with you?

How might they enhance the measurable business value your customer will receive?

How can you highlight the value of these processes and systems into your solutions?

How might they help you to differentiate yourself from your competitors?

To review the background information for this exercise, go to Chapter Eight.

APPLY THE PLAYBOOK – 16

Building the Solution – People

Review your high-potential customers and their strategic needs.

Identify those individuals in your organisation that have skills, experience and expertise relevant to your customers' needs.

Which individuals will provide your customers with high-class, specialist value?

What can you do to promote their specialised skills and talents to your customers?

How will you embed their expertise into your business solutions?

How can you leverage their expertise and create differentiation from your competitors?

To review the background information for this exercise, go to Chapter Eight.

APPLY THE PLAYBOOK – 17

Building the Solution – Partners

Review your high-potential customers and their strategic needs.

Identify those business partners with relevant products, processes and people.

How can they provide your customers with incremental and specialist value?

What can you do to promote their specialised capabilities to your customers?

How can you integrate their unique value into your business solutions?

How can you leverage their credentials and expertise and differentiate yourself from your competitors?

To review the background information for this exercise, go to Chapter Eight.

APPLY THE PLAYBOOK – 18

Building the Solution – Case Studies and Anecdotes

Review your high-potential customers and their strategic needs.

Where have you successfully delivered solutions in the past that met identical or similar needs?

Will those customers agree to be a referral or provide you with a testimonial?

Does your organisation have up-to-date and relevant case studies that you can use?

Who are the individuals in your customers' organisations who might be influenced by case studies and anecdotes?

How will you present the message to them?

To review the background information for this exercise, go to Chapter Eight.

Bibliography

Beckwith, Harry. *Selling the Invisible*. New York: Warner Books, 1997.

Bistritz, Stephen J and Read, Nicholas A C. *Selling to the C-Suite*. New York: McGraw-Hill, 2010.

Blessing, Buck. *Selling the Big Ticket*. Rocky Hill, NJ: Random Chance Press, 1994.

Cohen, Allan R and Bradford, David L. *Influence Without Authority*. New York: John Wiley & Sons, 1991.

Dixit, Avinash K. and Nalebuff, Barry J. *Thinking Strategically*. New York: W.W Norton & Co, 1993.

Geneen, Harold. *Managing*. London: Doubleday, 1984.

Hoffmann, Jeff and Finkel, David. *Seven Proven Principles to Grow Your Business and Get Your Life Back*. Penguin Group: New York, 2014.

Johnson, Larry. *Stop Selling, Start Partnering*. New York: John Wiley & Sons, 1995.

Krause, Donald G. *The Art of War for Executives*. New York: The Berkley Publishing Group, 1995.

Maister, David H. *True Professionalism.* New York: The Free Press, 1997.

McDonald, Malcolm, Rogers, Beth and Woodburn, Diana. *Key Customers – How to Manage Them Profitably.* Woburn, MA: Butterworth-Heinemann, 2000.

Page, Rick. *Hope Is Not a Strategy.* New York: Nautilus Press, 2002.

Rock, John. *Key Account Management.* Warriewood, Australia: Business and Professional Publishing, 1998.

Tzu, Sun. *The Art of War.* New York: Buccaneer Books, 1996.

Welch, Jack with Welch, Suzy. *Winning.* New York: HarperCollins Inc, 2005.

Lightning Source UK Ltd.
Milton Keynes UK
UKOW06f1532020316

269453UK00002B/120/P